GENOGRAMS
in Family Assessment

Monica McGoldrick
Randy Gerson

 W·W·NORTON & COMPANY New York·London

A NORTON PROFESSIONAL BOOK

Published simultaneously in Canada by Penguin Books Canada Ltd, 2801 John Street, Markham, Ontario L3R 1B4

Printed in the United States of America.

First Edition

Library of Congress Cataloging in Publication Data

McGoldrick, Monica.
  Genograms in family assessment.

  Bibliography: p.
  Includes index.
  1. Family psychotherapy – Technique.   2. Behavioral
assessment – Charts, diagrams, etc.   I. Gerson, Randy.
II. Title.   [DNLM: 1. Family.   2. Family Therapy.
3. Famous Persons.   WM 430.5.F2 M478g]
RC488.5.M395   1985   616.89'156   85-15269

ISBN 0-393-70002-X   PBK.
ISBN 0-393-70023-2

W. W. Norton & Company, Inc., 500 Fifth Avenue, New York, N.Y. 10110

W. W. Norton & Company Ltd., 37 Great Russell Street, London WC1B 3NU

1 2 3 4 5 6 7 8 9 0

To Murray Bowen, M. D., whose life work has been dedicated to the development of the family systems theory on which the interpretation of the genogram is based.

PREFACE

This book evolved out of a long interest in the clinical, research, and instructional value of genograms. We began by using genograms as a practical tool in family therapy and developed an interest in the potential of genograms, particularly computer-generated genograms, for data-based research. Through these interests we recognized a need for standardized genogram symbols and for a clear articulation of the assumptions underlying genogram interpretation and hypothesizing. Although hypothesizing about genograms is the bread and butter of many family therapists' work, it seems that many of the underlying assumptions have never been clarified. Our aim is to present a standard format for constructing the genogram and to clearly outline the principles underlying the interpretation and application of the genogram, so as to facilitate the use of this tool by family therapists, physicians, nurses, and other professionals working with families.

After deciding to develop a handbook for beginning students and a reference guide for those with more experience in the field, we struggled with how to make the subject interesting for readers at different levels. Genograms, which are fascinating to those who know the family members, remain meaningless squares and circles on a page to those who don't know the players in the drama. Our solution to this dilemma was to use primarily famous families rather than clinical cases to illustrate our points. We are family therapists, not historians, and thus the information we have been able to glean about these famous families is quite limited. Most of our sources have been biographies that could be found in libraries or bookstores. In fact, certain readers may know more about some of the families than we were able to track down from published sources. We apologize in advance for any inaccuracies that may occur. We hope that the material we have sketched will inspire readers to further pursue the fascinating stories of such families as the Freuds, Kennedys, Meads, Batesons, O'Neills, Adams, Roosevelts, Fitzgeralds and others. Surprisingly, only limited family descriptions are available of many of history's most interesting personalities. Perhaps future biographers will be more aware of family systems and use genograms to broaden their perspective on the individuals and families they describe.

ACKNOWLEDGMENTS

We are grateful to many people for their help in the development of this project. First of all we owe special thanks to our colleagues Michael Rohrbaugh and Howard Weiss, who struggled with us to develop the framework and ideas for this book, especially for challenging assumptions, the validity of which we took to be obvious, and for helping us clarify our thinking. Our editor, Susan Barrows, provided tireless help and care with us and with our manuscript, which made the task of completing the book a great deal easier. We also thank many others who contributed to the ideas and material in this book: Betty Carter, Neale McGoldrick, Robert Like, Fredda Herz, Cinda Kelly Graham, Devi Shah, Gena Strategos, Joyce Richardson, Froma Walsh, Carol Anderson, Helen McGoldrick, Meyer Rothberg, John Rogers, and David Reis, especially for his amazing endurance, good nature, and artistry in finishing the genograms.

Mary Scanlon, medical librarian at Rutgers, went out of her way time after time to provide us with materials we needed for this endeavor. We owe a special debt to Jeanine Stone and above all to Myra Wayton for their always cheerful efforts in the preparation of the manuscript.

Thanks also to Henry Murphree, Chairman of the Psychiatry Department at UMDNJ Rutgers Medical School and to Gary Lamson, the Director of its Community Mental Health Center for his good natured guidance, flexibility and support, which made work on this project possible. Thanks to Jack Saul, Douglas Siegal, David Forbes, Ginny Sherwood, Kathryn Maas, David Cohen, Tom Csaszar, Peter Mosely, and Pat Pogal for their friendship and support.

Special thanks to Joe and Evelyn and the whole Gerson family, who were always there. And thanks to Sophocles Orfanidis and to John Daniel Orfanidis, whose birth almost coincided with the birth of this book and whose coming adds a joyous new generation to our personal family genogram.

CONTENTS

LIST OF ILLUSTRATIONS

GENOGRAMS
in Family Assessment

1

WHY GENOGRAMS?

A genogram is a format for drawing a family tree that records information about family members and their relationships over at least three generations. Genograms display family information graphically in a way that provides a quick gestalt of complex family patterns and a rich source of hypotheses about how a clinical problem may be connected to the family context and the evolution of both problem and context over time.

In the following chapters, we outline our basic approach to genogram construction, present an outline for collecting genogram information in a family assessment, offer principles of genogram interpretation based on family systems theory, describe genogram applications in clinical practice, and finally, discuss the future potential of computerized genograms for family research. Along the way we use the genograms of various well-known families to enliven the subject.

Despite the widespread use of genograms by family therapists and physicians, there is no generally agreed-upon "right way" to do a genogram. Even among clinicians with similar theoretical orientations, there is only a loose consensus about what specific information to seek, how to record it, and what it all means. This book presents a standardized genogram format and describes the interpretive principles upon which genograms are based. Guidelines developed over the past ten or twelve years in collaboration with many colleagues are presented here as work in progress. They represent one way to do a genogram – a useful way, we believe – one which has been revised many times and will no doubt be revised again in the future.

Genograms are appealing to clinicians because they are tangible and graphic representations of a family. They allow the clinician to map the family structure clearly and to note and update the family "picture" as it emerges. For a clinical record, the genogram provides an efficient clinical summary, allowing a therapist unfamiliar with a case to grasp quickly a large amount of information about a family and to have a view of potential problems. While notes written in a chart or questionnaire answers may become lost in a clinical record, genogram information is immediately recognizable and can be added to and corrected at each clinical visit as more is learned about the family.

Genograms make it easier for a clinician to keep in mind family members, patterns and events that may have recurring significance in a family's ongoing care. Just as language potentiates and organizes our thought processes, family diagrams which map relationships and patterns of functioning may help clinicians think systemically about how events and relationships in their clients' lives are related to patterns of health and illness.

The information on a genogram is best understood from a systemic perspective. The genogram interview should be seen as one part of a comprehensive, systemic, clinical assessment. There is no quantitative measurement scale by which the clinician can use a genogram in a cookbook fashion to make clinical predictions. Rather, the genogram is a subjective interpretive tool with which the clinician can generate tentative hypotheses for further systemic evaluation.

Typically, the genogram is constructed in the first session and revised as new information becomes available. Thus, the initial assessment forms the basis for treatment. It is important to emphasize, however, that family therapists typically do not compartmentalize assessment and treatment. Each interaction of the therapist with the family informs the assessment and thus influences the next intervention.

Genograms can help family members see themselves in a new way and are thus an important way of "joining" with families in therapy. They enable an interviewer to reframe, detoxify, and normalize emotion-laden issues, creating a systemic perspective which helps to track family issues through space and time. Also, the genogram interview provides a ready vehicle for systemic questioning, which, in addition to providing information for the clinician, begins to orient the family to a systemic perspective. The genogram helps both the clinician and the family to see the "larger picture," both currently and historically; that is, the structural, relational, and functional information about a family on a genogram can be viewed both horizontally across the family context and vertically through the generations.

Scanning the breadth of the current family context allows the clinician to assess the connectedness of the immediate players in the family drama to each other, as well as to the broader system, and to evaluate the family's strengths and vulnerabilities in relation to the overall situation. Consequently, we include on the genogram the entire cast of characters — nuclear and extended family members as well as significant non-family members who have ever lived with or played a major role in the family's life — and a summary of the present family situation, including relevant events and problems. Current behavior and problems of family members can then be traced on the genogram from multiple perspectives. The index person (the person with the problem or symptom) may be viewed in the context of various subsystems, such as siblings, triangles, complementary and symmetrically reciprocal relationships, or in relation to the broader meta systems such as community, social institutions (schools, courts, etc.), and the broader sociocultural context.

By scanning the family system historically and assessing previous life cycle transitions, one can place present issues in the context of the family's evolutionary patterns. Thus, the genogram usually includes at least three generations of family members, as well as nodal and critical events in the family's history, particularly as related to the life cycle. When family members are questioned about the present situation in relation to the themes, myths, rules, and emotionally charged issues of previous generations, repetitive patterns become clear. Genograms "let the calendar speak" by suggesting possible connections between family events. Patterns of previous illness and earlier shifts in family relationships brought about through changes in family structure and other critical life changes can easily be noted on the genogram, providing a rich source of hypotheses about what leads to change in a particular family. (In conjunction with genograms, we usually include a family chronology, which depicts the family history in chronological order — see explanation on pp. 19-20.)

Genograms are most often associated with Bowen's family systems theory (Bowen, 1978; Carter & McGoldrick Orfanidis, 1976; Guerin & Pendagast, 1976; McGoldrick, 1977; Pendagast & Sherman, 1977; Bradt, 1980), but they are used by clinicians of other orientations as well (Hartman, 1978; Lieberman, 1979; Paul & Paul,

1974; Smoyak, 1982; Wachtel, 1982). In family therapy, genogram applications range from multigenerational mapping of the family emotional system using a Bowen framework, to systemic hypothesizing for Milan-style paradoxical interventions, to developing "projective" hypotheses about the workings of the unconscious from genogram interviews, to simply depicting the cast of characters in the family. Some family therapists have stressed the usefulness of genograms for keeping track of complex relational configurations seen in remarried families (McGoldrick & Carter, 1980; Sager et al., 1983), and for engaging and keeping track of information with families of certain ethnic backgrounds (Garcia Preto, 1982; Moitoza, 1982) and at certain points in the life cycle, such as later life.

Although structural and strategic family therapy theorists (Haley, 1976; Madanes, 1981; Minuchin, 1974) have not used genograms in their approaches, preferring to focus on the emotional relationships in the immediate family rather than on the biological and/or legal structure, they are nevertheless concerned about hierarchical structures, particularly coalitions where generational boundaries are crossed. The genogram can highlight both current and historical family patterns to illustrate these and other dysfunctional family structures.

Family physicians have used genograms to record family medical history efficiently and reliably (Jolly, Froom, & Rosen, 1980; Medalie, 1978; Mullins, & Christie-Seely, 1984; Rakel, 1977). They have, in fact, attempted to standardize genogram symbols (Jolly et al., 1980; McGoldrick, Froom & Snope, in preparation) and to develop efficient procedures for using genograms in medical practice (Rogers & Durkin, 1984).

Given the widespread use of the genogram by different family professionals, there is surprisingly little detailed information about its use, interpretation, and application. This book attempts to fill this gap. We begin by reviewing the systemic assumptions that guide us in using genograms in our work.

A FAMILY SYSTEMS PERSPECTIVE

The concept of system is used to refer to a group of people who interact as a functional whole. Neither people nor their problems exist in a vacuum. Both are inextricably interwoven with broader interactional systems, the most fundamental of which is the family.

The family is the primary and, except in rare instances, the most powerful system to which a person ever belongs. In this framework, "family" consists of the entire kinship network of at least three generations, both as it currently exists and as it has evolved through time (Carter & McGoldrick, 1980). The physical, social and emotional functioning of family members is profoundly interdependent, with changes in one part of the system reverberating in other parts of the system. In addition, family interactions and relationships tend to be highly reciprocal, patterned and repetitive. It is this redundancy of pattern that allows us to make tentative predictions from the genogram.

A basic assumption made here is that problems and symptoms reflect a system's adaptation to its total context at a given moment in time. The adaptive efforts of members of the system reverberate throughout many levels of a system—from the biological to the intrapsychic to the interpersonal, i.e., nuclear and extended family, community, culture and beyond (Bowen, 1978; Engel, 1980; Scheflen, 1981). Also, family behaviors, including problems and symptoms, derive further emotional and normative meaning in relation to both the sociocultural (Elder, 1977; McGoldrick, Pearce, & Giordano, 1982) and historical (McGoldrick & Walsh, 1983) context of the family. Thus, a systemic perspective involves understanding the problem on as many levels as possible.

Since the genogram has developed primarily out of the family systems theory of Murray Bowen (1978), the conceptual framework for analyzing genogram patterns has been based on his ideas. The following is for the most part derived from Bowen's work.

People are organized within family systems according to generation, age, and sex, to name a few of the most common factors. Where you fit in the family structure can influence your functioning, relational patterns, and the type of family you form for the next generation. Walter Toman (1976) has emphasized the importance of sex and birth order in shaping sibling relationships and characteristics. Given different family structural configurations mapped on the genogram, the clinician can tentatively predict likely personality characteristics and relational compatibility problems.

Families repeat themselves. What happens in one generation will often repeat itself in the next, i.e., the same issues tend to be played out from generation to generation, though the actual behavior may take a variety of forms. Bowen terms this the multigenerational transmission of family patterns. The hypothesis is that relationship patterns in previous generations could provide implicit models for family functioning in the next generation. On the genogram, we look for patterns of functioning, relationships and structure continuing or alternating from one generation to the next.

Clearly, this systems approach involves an understanding of both the current and historical context of the family. We agree with Carter (1978) that the "flow of anxiety" in a family system occurs along both vertical and horizontal dimensions. The "vertical" flow derives from patterns of relating and functioning that are transmitted historically down the generations, primarily through the process of emotional triangling. The "horizontal" flow of anxiety emanates from current stresses on the family as it moves forward through time, coping with the inevitable changes, misfortunes and transitions in the family life cycle. With enough stress on this horizontal axis, any family will experience dysfunction. Furthermore, stressors on the vertical axis may create added problems, so that even a small horizontal stress can have serious repercussions on the system. For example, if a young mother has many unresolved issues with her mother and/or father (vertical anxiety), she may have a particularly difficult time dealing with the normal vicissitudes of parenthood (horizontal anxiety). The genogram helps the clinician to trace the flow of anxiety down through the generations and across the current family context.

Given our historical perspective, we take a systemic view of the "coincidences" of events. Concurrent events in different parts of the family are not viewed as simply random happenings; rather, they are seen as often interconnected in a systemic way. In addition, critical events are more likely to occur at some times than at others, especially the nodal points of life cycle transition in a family's history. Symptoms tend to cluster around such transitions in the family life cycle, when family members face the task of reorganizing their relations with one another in order to go on to the next phase. The symptomatic family becomes stuck in time, unable to resolve its impasse by reorganizing and moving on. The history and relationship patterns revealed in a genogram assessment provide important clues about the nature of this impasse—how a symptom may have arisen to preserve or to prevent some relationship pattern or to protect some legacy of previous generations.

There are many types of relationship patterns in families. Of particular interest are patterns of relational distance. People may be very close or very distant or somewhere in between. At one extreme are family members who are very distant from or in conflict with each other. The family may actually be in danger of breaking up. At the other extreme is what is called emotional "fusion" or "stuck-togetherness" of individuals in the family system. Family members in fused or poorly differentiated relationships are vulnerable to dysfunction, which is assumed to occur when the level of stress or anxiety exceeds the system's capacity to deal with it. The more closed the boundaries of a system become, the more immune it is to input from the environment, and consequently, the more rigid family patterns become. In other words, family members in a closed, fused system react automatically to one another, practically impervious to events outside the system that require adaptation to changing conditions. Fusion may involve either positive or negative relationships; i.e., family members may feel very good about each other or experience almost nothing but hostility and conflict. In either case, there is an overdependent bond that ties the family together. With genograms clinicians can map family boundaries and indicate which family subsystems are fused and thus likely to be closed to new input about changing conditions.

As Bowen has pointed out, two-person relationships tend to be unstable. Under stress two people tend to draw in a third, stabilizing the system by forming a coalition, the two joining in relation to the third. The basic unit of an emotional system thus tends to be the triangle. As we shall see, genograms can help the clinician identify key triangles in a family system, see how triangular patterns repeat from one generation to the next, and design strategies for changing them.

Finally, as noted in our definition of system, the members of a system fit together as a functional whole. That is, the behaviors of different family members are complementary or reciprocal. This leads us to expect a certain interdependent fit or balance in families, involving give and take, action and reaction. Thus, a lack (e.g., irresponsibility) in one part of the family may be complemented by a surplus (overresponsibility) in another part of the family. The genogram helps the clinician pinpoint the contrasts and idiosyncrasies in families that indicate the type of complementarity or reciprocal balance.

A CAVEAT

Throughout this book, we make assertions about families based on their genograms. Let us remind you that our observations about these genograms are given only as tentative hypotheses. This is true for genogram interpretations in general. At best, they offer provocative suggestions for further exploration. Predictions based on the genogram are not fact. The principles for interpreting genograms should be seen as rules of thumb—nothing more.

In many of the genograms shown in this book, we provide more information than our discussion attempts to cover. We encourage readers to use these illustrative genograms as a departure point for further developing their own skills in using and interpreting genograms.

Clearly, a genogram is limited in how much information it can display. Clinicians gather a great deal more important information on people's lives than can ever appear on genograms. Therefore, genograms should never be used clinically out of context, as we do here for didactic purposes. The genogram is just one part of an ongoing clinical investigation and must be integrated into the total family assessment.

2

CONSTRUCTING GENOGRAMS

Genograms are part of the more general process of family assessment. In this chapter we will describe how to both construct a genogram and elicit relevant genogram information from a family during assessment.

CREATING A GENOGRAM

Creating a genogram involves three levels: 1) mapping the family structure, 2) recording family information, and 3) delineating family relationships.

Mapping the Family Structure

The backbone of a genogram is a graphic depiction of how different family members are biologically and legally related to one another from one generation to the next. This map is a construction of figures representing people and lines delineating their relationships. As with any map, the representation will have meaning only if the symbols are defined for those who are trying to read the genogram. Not surprisingly, there is a great deal of diversity in the way clinicians draw genograms. Different groups have their own favorite symbols and ways of dealing with complicated family constellations, which often leads to confusion in reading other clinicians' genograms. Recently a group of family physicians and family therapists (a Task Force of the North American Primary Care Research Group), chaired by McGoldrick, has collaborated to standardize the symbols and pro-

Male ☐   Female ◯

Diagram 2.1 Gender symbols

Male I. P. ▣   Female I. P. ◉

Diagram 2.2 Index person symbols

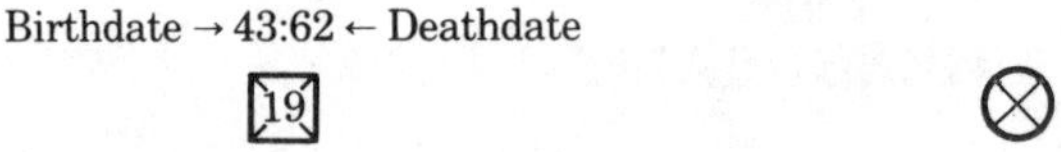

Birthdate → 43:62 ← Deathdate
⊠19   ⊗

Diagram 2.3 Birthdates and deathdates

cedures for drawing the genogram. These procedures form the basis for the guidelines presented here.

The family structure shows different family members in relation to one another. Each family member is represented by a box or circle according to his or her gender (Diagram 2.1). For the index person (or identified patient) around whom the genogram is constructed, the lines are doubled (Diagram 2.2). For a person who is dead, an X is placed inside the figure. Birth and death dates are indicated to the left and right above the figure (Diagram 2.3). The person's age at death is usually indicated within the figure. For example the male depicted here was born in 1943 and died in 1962 at the age of 19. In extended genograms that go back more than three generations, figures in the distant past are not usually crossed out, since they are presumably dead. Only relevant deaths are indicated in such genograms.

Pregnancies, miscarriages, abortions and stillbirths are indicated by other symbols (Diagram 2.4).

Diagram 2.4 Symbols for pregnancy, miscarrage, abortion and stillbirth

The figures representing family members are connected by lines that indicate their biological and legal relationships.

Two people who are married are connected by lines that go down and across, with the husband on the left and the wife on the right (Diagram 2.5). "M" followed by a date indicates when the couple was married. Sometimes only the last two digits of the year are shown (e.g., m.48) when there is little chance of confusion regarding the appropriate century. The marriage line is also the place where separations or divorces are indicated (Diagram 2.6). The slashes signify a disruption in the marriage – one slash for separation and two for a divorce.

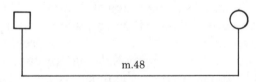

Diagram 2.5 Marriage connections

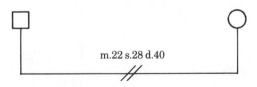

Diagram 2.6 Separations and divorces

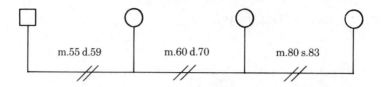

Diagram 2.7 A husband with several wives

Diagram 2.8 A wife with several husbands

Multiple marriages add a degree of complexity that is sometimes difficult to depict. Diagram 2.7 shows one way of indicating several wives of one husband, while Diagram 2.8 shows several husbands of one wife. The rule of thumb is that, when feasible, the different marriages follow in order from left to right, with the most recent marriage coming last. The marriage and divorce dates should also help to make the order clear. However, when each spouse has had multiple partners (and possibly children from previous marriages), mapping out the complex web of relationships can be very difficult indeed. One solution is to place the most recent relationship in the center and each partner's former spouses off to the side, as in Diagram 2.9.

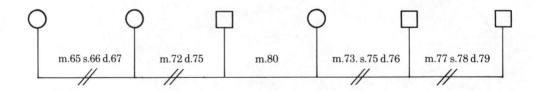

Diagram 2.9 Two partners who have each had multiple spouses

Diagram 2.10 Remarriages where each spouse has had several other partners

If previous spouses have had other partners, it may be necessary to draw a second line, slightly above the first marriage line, to indicate these relationships. In Diagram 2.10 each spouse has been married twice before. The husband's former wife had been married once before she married him, and she remarried afterwards. The wife's second husband has remarried since their divorce.

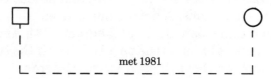

Diagram 2.11 Unmarried couple

If a couple are involved in a love affair or living together but not legally married, their relationship is depicted as with married couples, but a dotted line is used (Diagram 2.11). The important date here is when they met or started living together. (This may also be important information for married couples.)

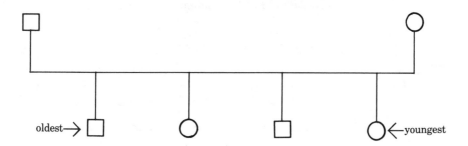

Diagram 2.12 Birth order

If a couple has children, then each child's figure hangs down from the line that connects the couple. Children are drawn left to right going from the oldest to the youngest, as in Diagram 2.12. If there

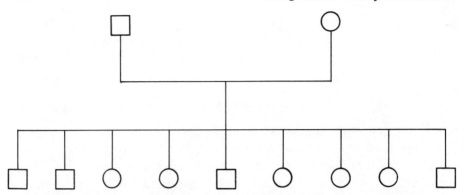

Diagram 2.13 Alternative method for depicting family with many children

are many children in a family, an alternate method (Diagram 2.13) may be used to save space. A dotted line is used to connect a foster or adopted child to the parents' line (Diagram 2.14). And finally, converging lines connect twins to the parental line. If the twins are identical, a bar connects them to each other (Diagram 2.15).

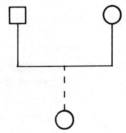

Diagram 2.14 Foster or adopted children

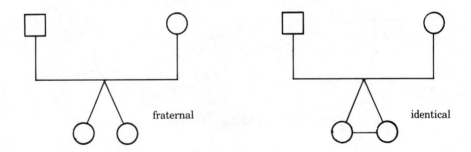

fraternal   identical

Diagram 2.15 Twins

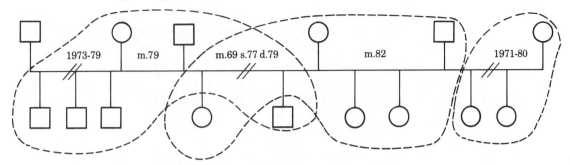

Diagram 2.16 Households of remarried families

Dotted lines are used to encircle the family members living in the immediate household. This is especially important in remarried families where children spend time in various households, as in the genogram shown in Diagram 2.16.

Now that we have the basic symbols and procedures for mapping the family structure on a genogram, let us put them into practice by using the family of a well-known celebrity of the psychiatric world: Sigmund Freud. Neither Freud nor his biographers ever did extensive research into his family and the details of his family life are sketchy. Nevertheless, we do know the basic structure of the Freud family.

First, we draw Sigmund's marriage to Martha and their children (Diagram 2.17).

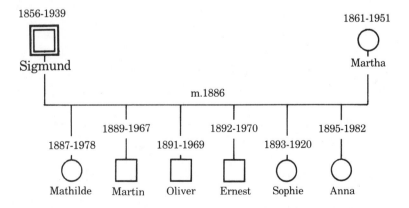

Diagram 2.17 Freud nuclear family

Next, we go back a generation and include both Sigmund's and Martha's parents and siblings (Diagram 2.18). In fact, we usually go back to the grandparents of the index person, including at least three generations on the genogram (four or even five generations if the index person has children and grandchildren).

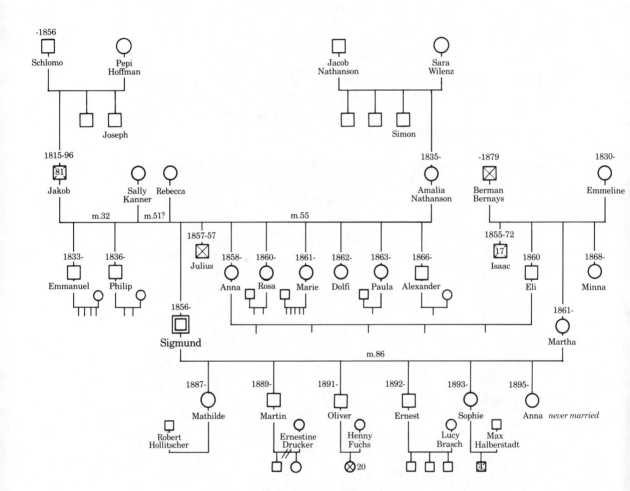

Diagram 2.18 Freud family – five generations

To highlight their central importance, the figures for Sigmund and Martha are lowered out of the sibling line. As can also be seen on this diagram, the spouses of siblings are also usually placed slightly lower than the siblings themselves, to keep the sibling patterns clear.

After the family structure has been drawn, the members of the household are encircled. Diagram 2.19 shows the Freud household in 1896, the year after their last child, Anna, was born, and the year that Sigmund's sister-in-law came to live with them.

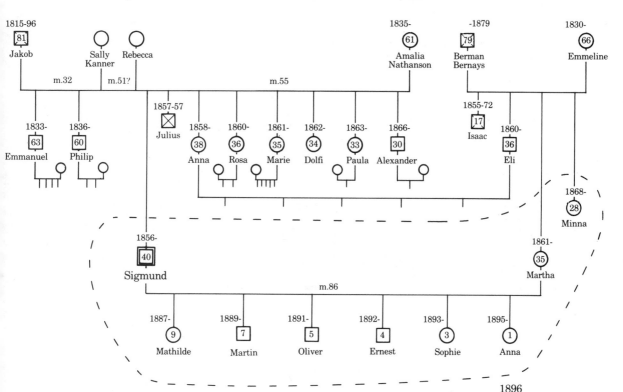

Diagram 2.19 Freud immediate household

The date in the bottom righthand corner tells the year when this genogram snapshot was taken. A clinician might use the genogram to freezeframe a moment in the past, such as the time of symptom onset or critical change in a family. When we choose one date in a person's life, other information, deaths, ages and important events are calculated in relation to that set date. It is then useful to put each person's age inside his or her figure. If the person is dead, the age at death is used instead. In Diagram 2.20, for example, we have somewhat arbitrarily chosen 1900, the year when Freud's first major book, *The Interpretation of Dreams*, was published. At that date there had been only a few deaths in the family – Sigmund's father, his brother Julius, and Martha's brother Isaac.

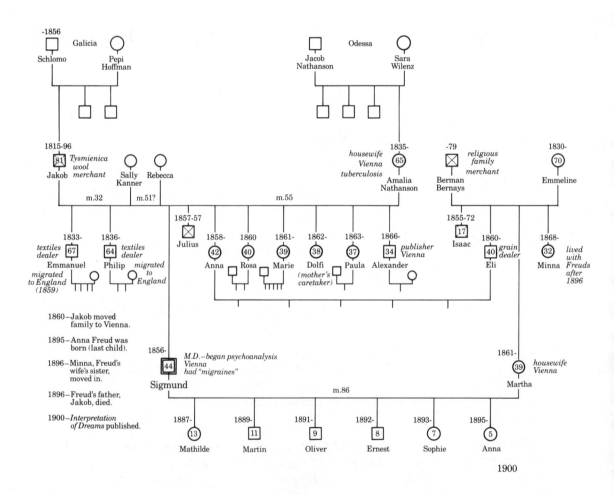

Diagram 2.20 Freud family with demographic, functioning, and critical event information.

When only partial information can be unearthed, that is included. For instance, Sigmund's father was married three times. We know that he had two children with his first wife, but little is known about his second wife, Rebecca (Clark, 1980; Glicklhorn, 1969). The third wife, of course, was Sigmund's mother, Amalia Nathanson.

Freud's is a relatively simple family to map. Unfortunately, not all families are so easy to show in simple graphic form. The numerous divorces and remarriages of many modern families and their complex biological and legal family relationships make drawing family structures a challenge. Later in this chapter we will discuss more complex family structures.

Recording Family Information

Once we have drawn the family structure, the skeleton of the genogram, we can start adding information about the family, particularly: a) demographic information; b) functioning information; and c) critical family events.

Demographic information includes ages, dates of birth and death, locations, occupations, and educational level.

Functional information includes more or less objective data on the medical, emotional and behavioral functioning of different family members. Objective signs, such as absenteeism from work and drinking patterns, may be more useful indications of a person's functioning than vague reports of problems by family members. Signs of highly successful functioning should also be included. The information collected on each person is placed next to his or her symbol on the genogram.

Critical family events include important transitions, relationship shifts, migrations, losses and successes. These give a sense of the historical continuity of the family and of the effect of the family history on each individual. Some of these events will have been noted as demographic data, e.g., family births and deaths. Others include marriages, separations, divorces, moves and job changes. Critical life events are recorded either in the margin of the genogram or, if necessary, on a separate attached page.

We generally keep a family chronology with the genogram. This is a listing in order of occurrence of important events in the family history that may have affected the individual. At times we make a special chronology for a critical time period, for example, to track a family member's illness in relation to other significant events. An individual chronology may also be useful for tracking a particular family member's life course (symptoms, functioning) within the context of the family.

Both the year and a brief description of each occurrence should be listed. For example, the following short list of critical events might appear on the Freud genogram:

1860   Jakob moved family to Vienna.
1895   Anna Freud was born (last child).
1896   Minna, Sigmund's wife's sister, moved in.
1896   Sigmund's father, Jakob, died.
1900   *Interpretation of Dreams* published.

When family members are unsure about dates, approximate dates should be given, preceded by a question mark, e.g., ?84 or ~84.

A more extensive chronology of family events could then be placed on a separate sheet of paper:

1855   Jakob Freud and Amalia Nathanson marry.
2/21/1856   Salamon Freud (Jakob's father) dies.
5/6/1856   Sigmund Freud is born in Freiberg.
4/1857   Julius Freud is born.
12/1857   Julius Freud dies.
1858   Anna Freud (Sigmund's sister) is born.
1860   Jakob moves his whole family to Vienna.
1866   Sigmund enters gymnasium (age 10).
1866   Alexander Freud is born (last child).
1873   Sigmund begins medical studies (age 17).
1879   Sigmund serves in military for 1 year.
1881   Sigmund receives medical degree (age 24).
1882   Sigmund becomes engaged to Martha Bernays.
1884   Sigmund publishes paper on cocaine.
1885   Sigmund attends Charcot lectures in Paris.
1886   Sigmund and Martha marry.
1889   Jean Martin Freud is born (first child).
1894   Sigmund's self-analysis begins.
1895   Anna Freud is born (last child).
1895   Sigmund publishes *Studies on Hysteria*.
1896   Minna, Sigmund's wife's sister, moves in.

1896   Jakob dies.
1900   Sigmund publishes *Interpretation of Dreams.*
1900   Sigmund ends self-analysis.
1902   Sigmund becomes Extraordinary Professor.

Clearly, a family chronology can vary in length and detail depending on the breadth and depth of the information available.

Let us look again at the Freud family genogram, with information on demographics, functioning, and critical events (Diagram 2.20, p. 18).

Showing Family Relationships

The third level of genogram construction is the most inferential. This involves delineating the relationships between family members. Such characterizations are based on the report of family members and direct observations. Different lines are used to symbolize the various types of relationship between two family members (Diagram 2.21). Although such commonly used relationship descriptors as "fused" or "conflictual" are difficult to define operationally and have different connotations for clinicians with various perspectives, these symbols are useful in clinical practice. Since relationship patterns can be quite complex, it is often useful to represent them on a separate genogram.

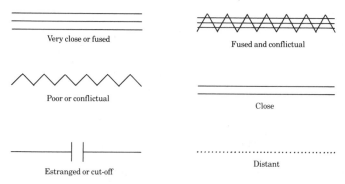

Diagram 2.21 Relationship lines

Again, the Freud family will be used to illustrate. Speculating on the relationship patterns of historical figures is a chancy business.

Without trying to justify our speculations, the genogram in Diagram 2.22 presents some of the *possible* relationship patterns that the available family background information on Freud suggests to us.

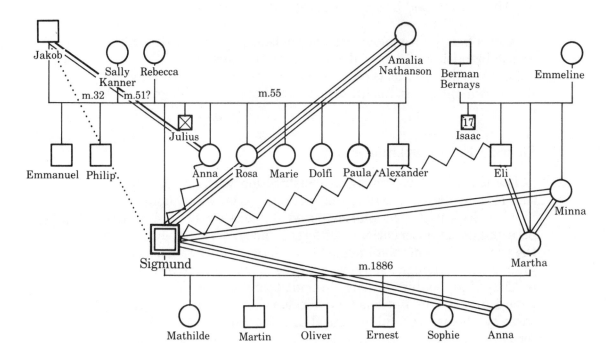

Diagram 2.22 Freud family – relationship patterns

COMPLEX GENOGRAMS

Genograms can become very complex and there is no set of rules that will cover all contingencies. We will show some of the ways we have dealt with a few common problems.

First, how do you plan ahead? Obviously, if you fill three-fourths of the page with father's three siblings, you will be stuck when you get to the mother and find she is the youngest of 12. It helps to get

an overview of the number of siblings and marriages in the parental generation before starting. The following questions will help you
plan and thus anticipate complexities from the start:

- How many times was each parent married?
- How many siblings did each parent have and where was he or she
  in the birth order?

For example, if you mapped the structure of Jane Fonda's family of origin, the basic framework would look like Diagram 2.23. The
genogram shows Jane's parents and grandparents. Each of her parents had had previous marriages and her father, Henry, had subse-
quent marriages. The other marriages are shown to the side of each
parent and are dated to indicate the order.

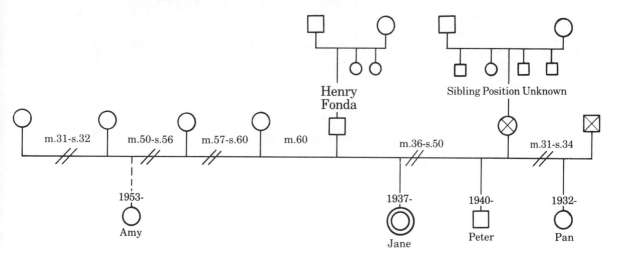

Diagram 2.23 Fonda family – basic structure

Generally, the focal point of the genogram is the index person and details about others in the genogram are shown as they relate to this person. The complexity of the genogram will thus depend on the depth and breadth of the information included. For example, if we were to include Jane's nuclear family, more detail on her mother's, father's, and sibling's various marriages, as well as the patterns of suicides, psychiatric hospitalizations and traumatic events, the genogram would look something like Diagram 2.24.

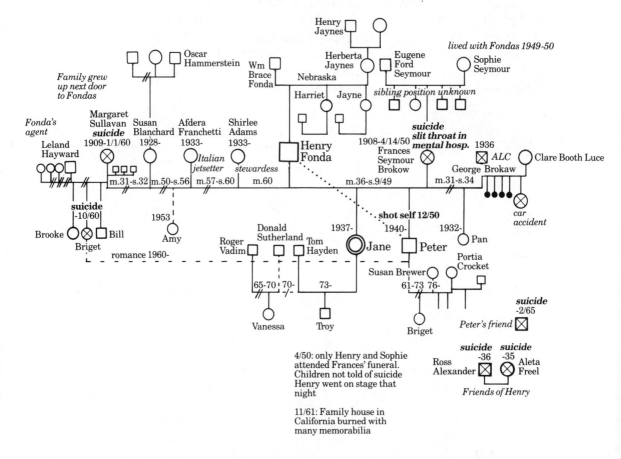

Diagram 2.24 Fonda family with details

This complex and crowded genogram reveals such important details as:

- Multiple marriages are common in this family.
- Both of Henry Fonda's first two wives committed suicide.
- Henry Fonda separated from his second wife, Jane's mother, only a few months before she committed suicide. He had already started an affair with his third wife, Susan Blanchard, whom he married eight months later.
- At the time of the third marriage (in fact, during the honeymoon), Peter Fonda, Jane's brother, shot himself (and nearly died).
- Henry Fonda had two close friends who committed suicide. His son, Peter, fell in love with Brigit Hayward the year that she killed herself, and also had a friend who committed suicide.

Nevertheless, there are limits to what the genogram can show, particularly regarding multiple marriages. Sometimes, in order to highlight certain points, the arrangement of the genogram structure is reorganized. For example, the Fonda family genogram has been arranged to highlight the ongoing relationship of the Haywards with the Fondas. Henry Fonda was married five times. His first wife, Margaret Sullavan, was married four times; Henry was her second husband. Margaret's third husband, Leland Hayward (who was also Henry Fonda's agent), was married five times, including twice to the same wife. Some of his spouses were also married numerous times, and so on.

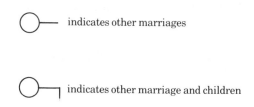

Diagram 2.25 Notation for additional information

Some complex family situations may require more than one page of genograms. It is important that the different genograms are connected in some way. Gerson has developed symbols (Diagram 2.25) to connect different genograms displayed on a computer (see Chapter 5). This notation can be used on any genogram to indicate that information about other marriage(s) and child(ren) can be found on another genogram.

Genograms are necessarily schematic and cannot detail all the vicissitudes of a family's history. For example, the Fonda genogram does not include the following information.

- Henry Fonda's first wife, Margaret Sullavan, lived very near the Fonda family in California with her third husband, Leland Hayward, Fonda's agent. After she separated from Leland Hayward, she moved with her children to Connecticut, where she lived very near the Fondas.
- Jane Fonda and Brook Hayward, Margaret's daughter, reportedly were best friends growing up and hoped that their parents would get back together again (Teichman, 1981, p. 132).
- Jane's mother's death was apparently kept from her and she only later found out about it in a movie magazine.
- Henry reportedly never discussed his wife's suicide with Peter and Jane.
- Henry Fonda and his mother-in-law held a private funeral for Jane's mother, which only they attended. Henry went on stage that same night.
- When Peter shot himself in the stomach during his father's third honeymoon in December 1950, eight months after his mother's suicide, Henry never asked Peter if he was upset about his mother's death (which Peter had been told was due to a heart attack).
- During Henry Fonda's fourth honeymoon in 1957, Peter got himself into such a bad state with drugs that his sister sent him to his aunt's in Nebraska. Henry had to return from his wedding trip to arrange for psychiatric treatment.
- Just after Henry Fonda's fifth honeymoon in 1965, Peter was involved in a drug arrest. His trial ended in a hung jury.

It is clear that Fonda family members have been greatly influenced by suicides and remarriages and that the Hayward and Fonda families were closely intertwined. Perhaps the extraordinary strength and force of personality that Peter and particularly Jane have shown in their careers reflect the many traumas they managed to overcome in their childhood. A comparable force was shown by Eleanor Roosevelt in response to many childhood traumas, as will be discussed later. Given the toxicity to families of suicide, the most traumatic of all deaths, the relevant facts surrounding the suicides would be critical to an understanding of the Fonda family. Such ad-

ditional family information that does not fit on a genogram should
be attached to it and noted by an asterisk.

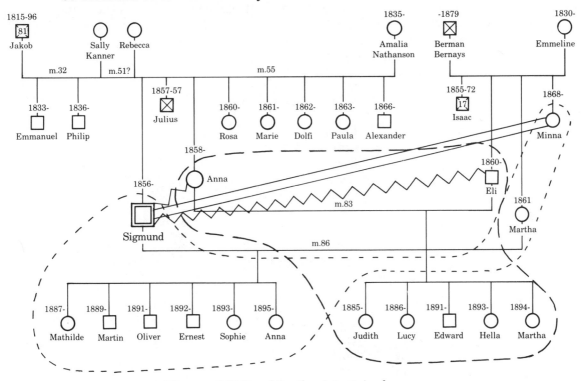

Diagram 2.26 Freud family – intertwined

Other problems arise where there are multiple intermarriages in
the family, e.g., cousins or stepsiblings marrying, or where children
have shifted residences many times to foster homes or various relatives or friends. There comes a point when the clinician must resort
to multiple pages or special notes on the genogram to clarify these
complexities.

Sometimes a genogram may be confusing because of the multiple connections between family members, as, for example, in the Sigmund Freud family (Diagram 2.26). Both Sigmund and his sister
Anna married siblings in the Bernays family, and the third living
Bernays sibling, Minna, was part of the Freud household from 1896
on. Marital lines are necessarily crossed in this genogram. In addition, the relationship lines show the conflicts and alliances that
reflect the merger of these two families. For an example of an even
more intertwined family, see the Jefferson family in Chapter 3 (p. 68).

Genograms may become complex when children have been adopted
or raised in a number of different households as in Diagram 2.27,
where the genogram shows as much of the information on the transitions and relationships as possible. In such cases let practicality
and possibility be your guides. Sometimes the only feasible way to
clarify where children were raised is to take chronological notes on
each child.

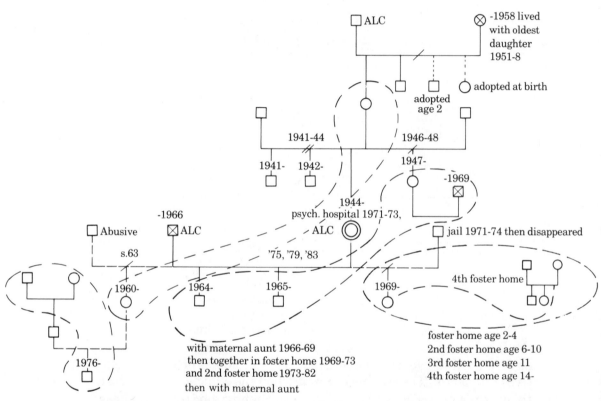

Diagram 2.27 Family with children living in other households and foster homes

Finally, there may be a problem with discrepant information. For
example, what happens if three different family members give different dates for a death or conflicting descriptions of family relationships? The best rule of thumb is to note important discrepancies

whenever possible. In Diagram 2.28, each son has given a different report of the date of the father's death and of who is closer to their mother. Bradt (1980) uses color-coded genograms to distinguish the source of information, although this method might seem impossibly cumbersome to many clinicians.

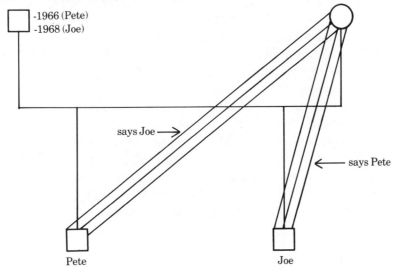

-1966 (Pete)
-1968 (Joe)

says Joe →

← says Pete

Pete   Joe

Diagram 2.28 Discrepant information

In sum, large, complex families with multiple marriages, intertwined relationships, many transitions and shifts, and/or multiple perspectives challenge the skill and ingenuity of the clinician trying the draw a genogram within a finite space. Improvisation and additional pages are often needed.

THE GENOGRAM INTERVIEW

Gathering information for the genogram usually occurs in the context of a family interview. Unless family members come in specifically to tell their family history for research purposes, you cannot simply gather genogram information and ignore the family's agenda for the interview. Such single-mindedness will not only hinder you in getting pertinent information, but also alienate the family from treatment. Gathering family information and constructing the genogram should be part of the more general task of joining and helping the family.

The Rashomon Effect

Genogram information can be obtained by interviewing one family member or several. Clearly, getting information from several family members increases reliability and provides the opportunity to compare perspectives and observe interactions directly. Often, when we interview several family members, we get what we call the *Rashomon* effect, based on a famous Japanese movie where one event is shown from the perspective of a number of different characters. Similarly, we find in genogram interviews that family members tell different stories about the same events.

Of course, seeing several family members is not always feasible, and the interview described here can also be used with one person. The time required to complete a genogram assessment can vary greatly. While the basic information can usually be collected in less than half an hour, a comprehensive family assessment interview involving several family members may take from 60 to 90 minutes. Some clinicians prefer to spread the interviewing over a number of sessions.

The Family Information Net

The process of gathering family information can be thought of as casting out a metaphorical information net in larger and larger circles in order to capture relevant information about the family and its broader context. The net spreads out in a number of different directions:

- from the presenting problem to the larger context of the problem.
- from the immediate household to the extended family and broader social systems.
- from the present family situation to a historical chronology of family events.
- from easy, nonthreatening queries to difficult, anxiety-provoking questions.
- from obvious facts to judgments about functioning and relationships to hypothesized family patterns.

The Presenting Problem and the Immediate Household

Family members usually come with specific problems, which should be the clinician's starting point. At the outset, we tell families that we need some basic information about them to fully understand the problem. Such information usually grows naturally out of exploring the presenting problem and its impact on the immediate household. It makes sense to most people for the clinician to ask about the immediate family and the context in which the problem occurs:

- Who lives in the household?
- How is each person related?
- Where do other family members live?

The clinician asks the name, age, and sex of each person in the household in order to sketch the immediate family structure. Other revealing information can be elicited through inquiring about the problem:

- Which family members know about the problem?
- How does each view it, and how has each of them responded?
- Has anyone in the family ever had similar problems?
- What solutions were attempted by whom in those situations?

This is also a good time to inquire about previous efforts to get help for the problem, including previous treatment, therapists, hospitalizations, and the current referral source.

The Current Situation

Next the clinician spreads the information net into the current family situation. This line of questioning usually follows naturally from questions about the problem and who is involved:

- What has been happening recently in your family?
- Have there been any recent changes in the family (people coming or leaving, illnesses, job problems, etc.)?

It is important to inquire about recent life cycle transitions as well as anticipated changes in the family situation (especially exits and entries of family members — births, marriages, divorces, deaths, the departure of family members, etc.).

The Wider Family Context

The clinician should look for an opportunity to explore the wider family context by asking about the extended family of all the adults involved. At a point in the discussion when the family seems at ease, the interviewer might say something like, "I would now like to ask you something about your background to help make sense of your present problem."

When family members react negatively to questions about the extended family or complain that such matters are irrelevant, it makes sense to redirect the focus back to the immediate situation, until the connections between the present situation and other family relationships or experiences can be established. Gentle persistence over time will usually result in obtaining the information.

The clinician should inquire about each side of the family separately, beginning, for example, with the mother's side:

- Let's begin with your mother's family. Your mother was which one of how many children?
- When was she born?
- Is she alive?
- (If not), when did she die? What was the cause of her death?
- (If alive), where is she now? What does she do?
- Is she retired? When did this happen?
- When and how did your mother meet your father? When did they marry?
- Had she been married before? (If so), when? Did she have children by that marriage? Did they separate or divorce or did the spouse die? If so, when was that?

And so on. In like fashion, the same series of questions is asked about the father. Then the clinician might ask about each parent's family of origin, i.e., father, mother, and siblings. The goal is to get information about at least three or four generations, including grandparents, parents, aunts, uncles, siblings, spouses, and children of the IP. The information net should extend beyond the biological and legal structure of the family to encompass common law and cohabiting relationships, miscarriages, abortions, stillborns, foster and adopted children.

The Social Context

Inquiries should be made regarding friends, clergy, caretakers, teachers, doctors, etc., who are important to the functioning of the family, and this information should also be included on the genogram. In exploring outside supports for the family, the clinician might ask the following:

- What roles have outside people played in your family?
- Have you gotten help from the community?
- Who outside the family has been important in your life?
- Has anyone else ever lived with your family? When? Where are they now?
- What has been your family's experience with doctors and other helping professionals or agencies?

The Facts

In fleshing out the nuclear and extended families, the initial concern should be with getting the "facts" on each family member. These are the vital statistics of the family, the type of objective data that usually could be verified by public record. The goal is to obtain the following for each family member:

- dates of birth, marriage, separation, divorce, illness, and death (including cause);
- sibling position;
- ethnic and religious background;
- occupation and education;
- current whereabouts.

The Historical Perspective

As the clinician collects more and more "facts" about family events, certain gaps will appear in the history. To get a broad historical perspective on the family, the clinician uses the genogram to map the family's evolution through time. If the family appears receptive, the clinician may start one or more family members on a project of historical research in order to expand this perspective. Family members are encouraged to seek more information by speaking to other relatives, consulting family bibles, or obtaining medical or genealogical records.

The goal is not only to track important family events, but also to locate the family's development in historical time. For example, a suicide in 1929 suggests certain hypotheses (depression related to the stock market crash); a marriage in 1941 suggests other historical circumstances which would influence a couple's development (the husband's involvement in World War II).

There are certain critical life events that may be important to explore in detail.

- How did the family react when a particular family member was born? Who attended the christening ceremony or bris? Who was named after whom and who "should have been"?
- How did the family react when a particular family member died? Who took it the hardest? The easiest? Who attended the funeral? What was the effect when the will was read? Who wasn't there who "should have been"?
- When and why did the family migrate to this country? How many generations of the family have lived here? How well did the initial generations fare? Which members of the immigrant generation learned the language?

Tracking shifts that occurred around births, deaths and other transitions can lead the clinician to hypotheses about the family's adaptive style. Particularly critical are untimely or traumatic deaths and the deaths of pivotal family members. We look for specific patterns of adaptation or rigidification following such transitions. Assessment of past adaptive patterns, particularly families' response to and reorganization after losses and other critical transitions, are often crucial in helping a family (McGoldrick & Walsh, 1983). A family's past and the relationship family members have to it provide important clues about family rules, expectations, and patterns of organization.

The history of specific problems should also be investigated in detail. The focus should be on how family patterns have changed at different periods: before the problem began, at the time of onset, at the time of first seeking help, and at the present. Asking about how the family sees the future of the problem is also informative. Questions include:

- When did the problem begin? Who noticed it first? Who thought it was serious or not serious?

- Were family relationships different before the problem began? What other problems existed?
- Does the family see the problem as having changed? In what ways? For better or for worse?
- What will happen in the family if the problem continues? If it goes away? What does the future look like? What changes do family members imagine are possible in the future?

Seeing the family in its historical perspective involves linking past, present and future and noting the family's flexibility in adapting to changes.

Tracking Family Relationships and Roles

While mapping on the genogram the nuclear and extended family and gathering facts on different family members, the clinician should also begin to make inquiries and judgments about the different types of relationships family members have and the functioning and roles of each person in the family. This involves going beyond the bare facts to clinical judgment and acumen. Inquiries about family relationships, functioning and roles can touch sensitive nerves in the family and should be made with care. Questions on relationships include:

- Are there any family members who do not speak to each other or who have ever had a period of not speaking? Are there any who were/are in serious conflict?
- Are there any family members who are extremely close? Who helps out when help is needed? In whom do family members confide?
- All couples have some sort of marital difficulties. What sorts of problems and conflicts have you encountered? What about your parents' and siblings' marriages?
- How do you each get along with each child? Have any family members had particular problems dealing with their children?

The clinician should get as many perspectives on family relationships as possible. For example, the husband may be asked, "How close do you think your mother and your older brother were?" Then the wife is asked for her impression of that relationship. The goal is to uncover differences, as well as agreements, about family relationships and to use the different perceptions of the family to enrich the genogram picture for both the therapist and the family.

From the relationships between family members, the clinician also begins to get a sense of the complementarity of roles in the family. Questions that elucidate the role structure include:

- Has any family member been focused on as the caretaker? The problematic one? The "sick" one? The "bad" one? The "mad" one?
- Who in the family is seen as the strong one? The weak one? The dominant one? The submissive one?
- Who in the family is seen as the successful one? The failure?
- Who is seen as warm? As cold? As caring? As distant?

Labels or nicknames used by family members are particularly instructive. Often, each family member has a family-wide label that describes and even circumscribes his or her position in the family (e.g., the "tyrant," the "supermother," etc.). Labels are thus good clues to the emotional patterns in the system (Papp, Silverstein, & Carter, 1973).

Sometimes it is useful to ask how members of the present family would be characterized by other family members, e.g., "How do you think your older brother would describe your relationship with your wife?" or "How would your father have described you when you were 13, the age of your son now?" Again, gathering as many perspectives as possible enriches the family's view of itself, and introducing differences provides channels for new information.

Difficult Questions About Individual Functioning

Assessment of individual functioning may or may not involve much clinical judgment. Alcohol abuse, chronic unemployment and severe symptomatology are facts that directly indicate poor functioning. However, many family members may function well in some areas but not in others or may cover up their dysfunction. Often, it takes careful questioning to reveal the true level of functioning.

Questions about individual functioning may be difficult or painful for family members to answer and must be approached with sensitivity and tact. The family members should be warned that the questions may be difficult and perhaps told to let the clinician know if an area is being touched that they prefer not to discuss. The clinician will need to judge the degree of pressure to apply if the family resists such questions.

Serious Problems

- Has anyone in the family had a serious medical or psychological problem? Been depressed? Had anxieties? Fears? Lost control? Has there been physical or sexual abuse? Are there any other problems that worry you?
- When did that problem begin? Did you seek help? If so, when? What happened? What is the status of that problem now?

Work History

- Have there been any recent job changes? Unemployment? Do you like your job? Who else works? Do they like it?
- How much income is there? How does the economic situation compare with that of your relatives?

Drugs and Alcohol

- Do any family members routinely use medication? What kind and for what?
- Do you think any members drink too much or have a drug problem? Has anyone else ever thought so? What drugs? When? What has the family done about it?

Trouble With the Law

- Have any family members ever been arrested? For what? When? What was the result? What is that person's legal status now?
- Has anyone ever lost his or her driver's license?

Setting Priorities for Organizing Genogram Information

As we will see in the next chapter, information gathered for the genogram often reveals family patterns which clinicians interpret and utilize in clinical practice. In the process of gathering the information, the clinician should be aware of the type of patterns that may appear and probe for further information when such patterns are suggested by the data.

One of the most difficult aspects of genogram assessment remains the problem of setting priorities for inclusion of family information

on a genogram. Clinicians cannot follow every lead that the genogram interview may suggest. Awareness of basic genogram patterns
can help the clinician set such priorities. As a rule of thumb, the data
are scanned for the following:

- Repetitive symptom, relationship or functioning patterns seen
  across the family and over the generations. Repeated triangles,
  coalitions, cut-offs, patterns of conflict, over- and under-functioning
  are central to genogram interpretation.
- Coincidences of dates: e.g., the death of one family member or anniversary of this death occurring at the same time as symptom
  onset in another, or the age at symptom onset coinciding with the
  age of problem development of another family member.
- The impact of change and untimely life cycle transitions: changes
  in functioning and relationships that correspond with critical family
  life events. Of particular interest are untimely life cycle transitions,
  e.g., births, marriages, or deaths that occur "off schedule" (Neugarten, 1970).

Being aware of possible patterns makes the clinician more sensitive to what is missing. Such missing information about important family members or events and discrepancies in the information
offered frequently reflect charged emotional issues in the family. The
clinician should take careful note of the connections family members
make or fail to make to various events.

3

INTERPRETING GENOGRAMS

The interpretive principles for evaluating genograms have never been stated explicitly, although the underlying assumptions, based on the principles of family systems theory, are familiar to many clinicians. We have simplified the underlying principles of genogram interpretation for didactic purposes; they will undoubtedly require much refinement in the future. For further elaboration of ideas only summarized here, the reader is referred to the concepts of Bowen theory (Bowen, 1978), Toman's (1976) ideas about sibling constellation, and the writings of other family theorists (such as Fogarty, 1973; Friedman, 1985; Guerin, 1976; Hoffman, 1981). The following discussion is meant only to suggest some possible ways of viewing genograms rather than to exhaustively list all of the complex factors which must be considered in interpreting them.

Each category discussed in this chapter represents a general set of assumptions from which one generates clinically relevant working hypotheses about family patterns. Although we will present each category as involving distinct inferential processes, the categories often overlap with one another. This is to be expected since the categories are based on systemic assumptions that are theoretically connected.

CATEGORY 1: FAMILY STRUCTURE

The first area of exploration on a genogram is the basic family structure; that is, what are the structural patterns that connect the lines and figures on the family diagram? Examining this graphic family structure allows one to make hypotheses about likely family issues, roles, and relationships based on normative expectations for household composition, sibling constellations, and unusual family configurations.

Household Composition

One glance at the structure of the genogram usually tells the clinician the family's composition, i.e., whether there is an intact nuclear family household, a single-parent household, a remarried family, a three-generational household, or a household including extended family members.

Intact Nuclear Family Household

In the United States, this is often thought of as the "typical" traditional family, though its prevalence is statistically declining. In 1983 it represented only 29% of U.S. households (Glick, 1984). On the genogram the structure appears as spouses married for the first time and their biological children (Diagram 3.1).

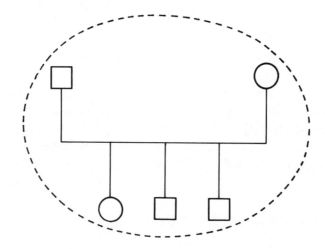

Diagram 3.1 Intact nuclear family household

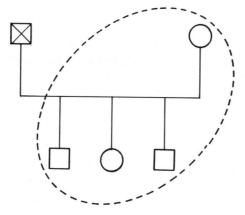

Diagram 3.2 One parent deceased

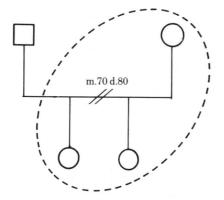

Diagram 3.3 One parent has left

In itself this family structure usually does not attract the clinician's attention. However, if the family is under severe stress or there is a great deal of marital conflict, one might begin to explore what factors and strengths have helped to keep this family together. In addition, intact families can be expected to have the usual parent-child triangles (see Category 5, Relational Patterns and Triangles).

Single-parent Household

A single-parent household is one in which only one parent is raising the children. This may be due to the death of one of the parents (Diagram 3.2). Or it may have resulted from the departure of one of the parents due to divorce, separation or desertion (Diagram 3.3).

Seeing a single-parent structure on the genogram should cue the clinician to explore all the issues of being a single parent: the loneliness, economic problems, the difficulties in raising children alone, etc. Also of interest would be the impact on the family (particularly the children) of the loss of one of the parents (see Category 4, Life Events and Family Functioning) and the relational patterns and triangles typical of this family situation (see Category 5). Often such households are part of larger networks, sometimes called binuclear families (Ahrons, 1980), which may need to be called "multi-nuclear families," in which children are part of several different family structures.

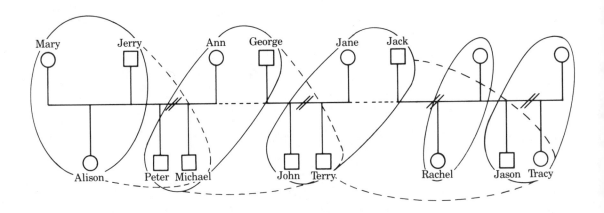

Diagram 3.4 Family with children participating in different households

In the family shown in Diagram 3.4 John and Terry usually live with their mother, Jane, and her boyfriend, Jack. At times, Jack's children, Rachel by his first wife and Jason and Tracy by his second wife, come for vacations and weekends. At other times John and Terry go to stay with their father, George, who lives with his girlfriend, Ann. During the school year, Ann's two sons, Peter and Michael, also live with them. During vacations, however, Peter and Michael go to stay with their own father, Jerry, his new wife, Mary, and his new daughter, Alison. Clearly, it can be difficult to map the fluctuating living arrangements in such families.

Remarried Family

A remarried family is a family where one or both parents have remarried following a divorce or death, bringing into the household a stepparent. The children of the previous marriages may all live in the same household or be split between the different households, as in Diagram 3.5.

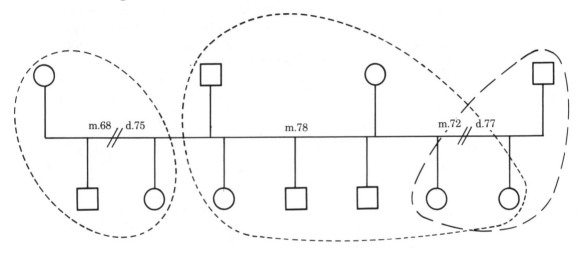

Diagram 3.5 Remarried family

Remarried families have to deal with particular issues: custody, visitation, jealousy, favoritism, loyalty conflict, stepparent and stepsibling problems, etc. The clinician should also explore the impact of the divorce and remarriage on each family member (see Category 4, Life Events and Family Functioning) and the relational patterns and triangles inherent in this type of family situation (see Category 5).

Three-generational Household

In a three-generational household the parent(s) live with the grand-parent(s) on one side of the family. This is particularly common for single parents where, for example, a mother might live with her mother for aid and support, as in Diagram 3.6. Here the father has left his wife and children and then the mother and her sons have moved in with the grandmother, whose other daughter also lives in the household. With a three-generational household the clinician should explore issues around cross-generational boundaries, alliances and conflicts, asking, for example, who does the parenting. Also of interest would be the relational patterns and triangles inherent in three-generational households (see Category 5).

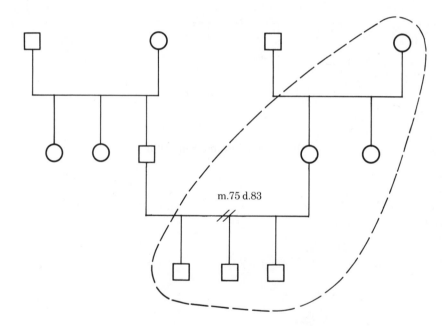

Diagram 3.6 Three-generational household

Households Including Extended Family and Non-family Members

Housekeepers, sisters, brothers, aunts, uncles, cousins, foster children, and adopted children may be included in the household.

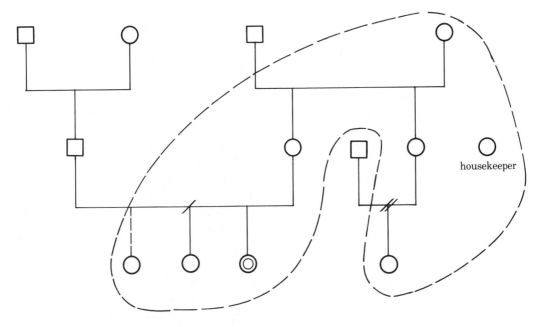

Diagram 3.7 Household with non-nuclear family members

The household in Diagram 3.7, for example, includes an aunt, a cousin, a housekeeper, and an adopted child. Ethnic groups vary tremendously in their definitions of family (McGoldrick, 1982) and it is important to attend to structures that include godparents or other kinship networks and to assess how the relationship patterns may be affected by these structures. When a housekeeper, close friend or other "outsider" is especially important to the family, he or she often becomes a member of the informal extended kinship network (Stack, 1974) and should be included in the genogram.

The clinician should explore the roles and relationships of extended family members living in the household. The issues will vary according to their relational position. A spouse's brother, sister, aunt, uncle or cousin may seem like an intruder to the other spouse (see Category 5 for discussion of in-law triangles), while foster and adopted children often become involved in predictable relational patterns (see Category 5). It is important to consider the reverberations in both the immediate and extended family of the entry of an extended family member or other person into the household (see Category 4, Life Events and Family Functioning).

Sibling Constellation

The importance of birth position, sex, and number of years in age from other siblings has long been discussed in the literature, although there has not always been agreement on the role sibling constellation plays in development (Adler, 1958; Bank & Kahn, 1982; Ernst & Angst, 1983; Forer, 1976; Sutton-Smith & Rosenberg, 1970; Toman, 1976). Many factors come into play that influence the role of sibling patterns. Ethnic groups vary in the role that sibling position plays in the family. In addition, under certain circumstances, such as chronic family disruption, siblings may become each other's main protector and resource (Bank & Kahn, 1982). At present, sibling patterns are undergoing significant changes, primarily because of different child-bearing and child-rearing patterns that have followed the increased availability of birth control, the women's movement, the entry of more women into the work force, and changing family structures. Couples are having fewer children and children are spending more of their time in daycare and other nonsibling groups, as well as in remarried families, where their sibling position and role often change. These factors all complicate our understanding of sibling patterns in a family. Nevertheless, for most of us sibling relationships are the longest relationships we have in life. We will venture some hypotheses about typical sibling patterns, which are especially evident when mapped on a genogram. These hypotheses derive primarily from the work of Walter Toman (1976).

Birth Order

Sibling position can have particular relevance for one's emotional position in the family of origin and future relations with a spouse and children. For example, an oldest child is more likely to be over-responsible, conscientious and parental, while the youngest is more likely to be child-like and carefree.

Often, oldest children will feel they are special and particularly responsible for maintaining the family's welfare or carrying on the family tradition. Consequently, they may feel they have a heroic mission to fulfill in life. In addition, sometimes the oldest will resent younger siblings, feeling they are an intrusion on his or her earlier exclusive possession of the parents' love and attention.

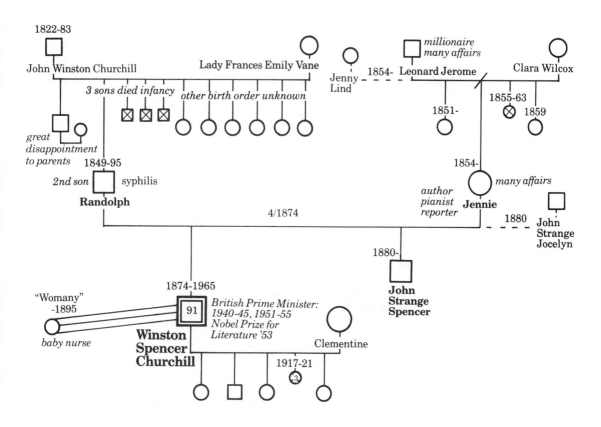

Diagram 3.8 Churchill family

Winston Churchill (Diagram 3.8) in many way fits the stereotype of an oldest son. He was a man with a special sense of himself and his responsibility. As Piers Brendon, one of Churchill's biographers, has said:

> Churchill's personality was formed on heroic lines. It was a monstrous compound of courage, energy, imagination, tenacity, humour, compassion; and of ambition, impatience, volatility, obsessiveness, egotism, brutality . . . he always saw himself through the basilisk eye of history as a man of destiny bestriding his age like a colossus. And so powerful was his personality, so compelling his eloquence, that he managed to make others share this glittering vision. (1984, p. 2)

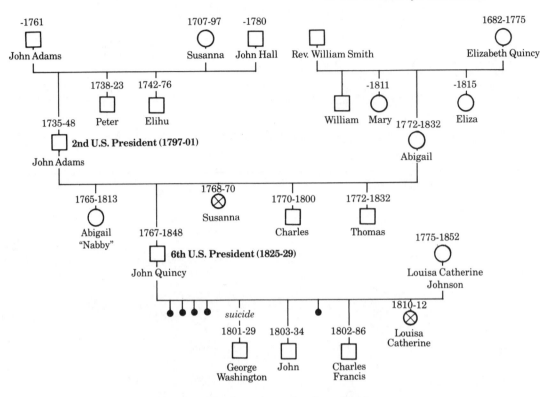

Diagram 3.9 The Adams family — oldest sons

Great things are often expected of a firstborn. The Adams family (Diagram 3.9) is a good example of this tendency. John Adams, the second President of the United States, was himself an oldest. We know little of the expectations of his parents but we do know that he had the high ambition, drive and sense of responsibility so typical of an oldest child. He passed these expectations down to his oldest son, John Quincy Adams. (Although John Quincy had an older sister, apparently less was expected of her — see discussion below on sexual biases.) The father was very straightforward in what he wanted from his son:

> You come into life with advantages which will disgrace you if your success is mediocre. And if you do not rise to the head not only of your Profession, but of your Country, it will be your own Lasiness, Slovenliness, and Obstinacy (sic). (Nagel, 1983, p. 53)

John Quincy did become President of the United States, but paid a price for being the object of such great expectations. He was filled with self-doubt and self-criticism, periodically depressed, and, as his wife described him, characterized by "unnecessary harshness and severity of character" (Nagel, 1983, p. 65). Sometimes, the oldest suffers severely under the pressure to excel, as did John Quincy's oldest child, George Washington, who did quite poorly in life and eventually committed suicide. George was born after four miscarriages, a series of events which would be likely to make the birth of the first child even more important to the parents.

The youngest, on the other hand, is often treated as the "baby" in the family and may be used to having others take care of him or her. The youngest may feel more carefree and less burdened by family responsibility, and often has less respect for authority and convention.

George Bernard Shaw, the famous playwright, is a good illustration of a youngest child. In fact, he was the youngest son of a youngest son (see p. 54). Shaw was always the rebel and iconoclast. He used humor to poke fun at convention and institutions and was less interested in creating order than in making fun of order that he considered unnecessary. In day-to-day life, he took very poor care of himself. This changed only when at age 42 he married Charlotte Payne-Townshend, an oldest, who was quite bothered by the untidy way he lived.

Only children (Falbo, 1984; Jacobus, in preparation), not surprisingly, tend to be more socially independent, less oriented toward peer relationships, more adultlike in behavior at an earlier age, and perhaps more anxious at times as a result of the attention and protectiveness of their parents. They presumably mix characteristics of both the oldest and the youngest, but seem to take on more of the characteristics of the oldest, being the sole focus of the parents' attention.

Indira Gandhi, the second Prime Minister of India, is an example of an only child (Diagram 3.10). She grew up quite isolated and lived primarily in the presence of older people, early becoming her father's confidante. She clearly had the sense of mission and responsibility of an oldest, but as a leader, as befits an only child, she was autocratic and led a rather isolated existence, keeping her own counsel. Of interest is the fact that both her father and paternal grandfather were functional only children. Her father, Jawaharlal Nehru, was eleven years older than his next sibling and his father, Motilal Nehru, also a leader of India, was much younger than his siblings and raised in the home of his older brother, because his father had died before he was born. The illnesses of both Jawaharlal's mother and Indira's mother may also have compounded the independence of their roles as only children.

Being the sole focus of attention, only children often have very close attachments to their parents throughout their lives. This was the case with Franklin Roosevelt (see p. 52). Although he actually had a half-brother, Franklin Roosevelt was raised as an only son because his brother was 28 years older. As is common in such situations, his mother doted on him, particularly after his father died when he was quite young. To his wife Eleanor's chagrin, he remained quite attached to his mother throughout his life.

Sibling position may predict some marital difficulties. For example, Toman predicts that those who marry a spouse in the same sibling position will have more difficulty adjusting to marriage. He believes that couples who come from complementary sibling positions, for whom the marriage repeats their sibling constellation, will have an easier time, all things being equal.

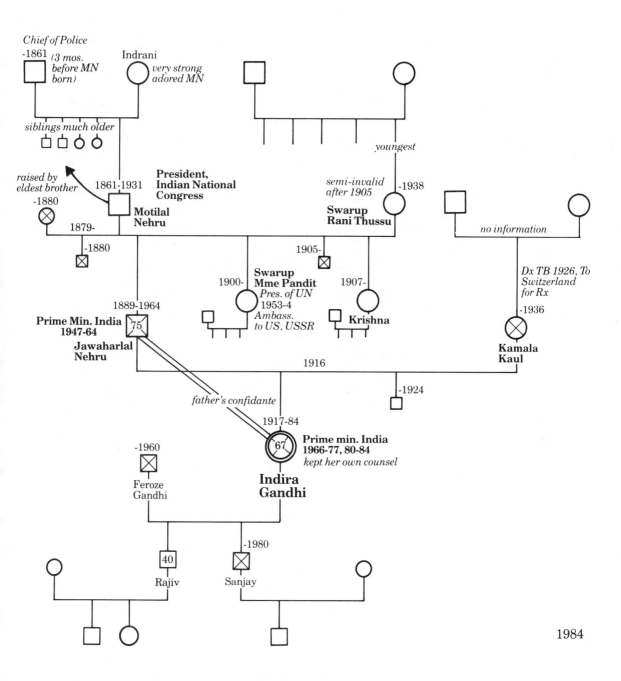

Diagram 3.10 Indira Gandhi

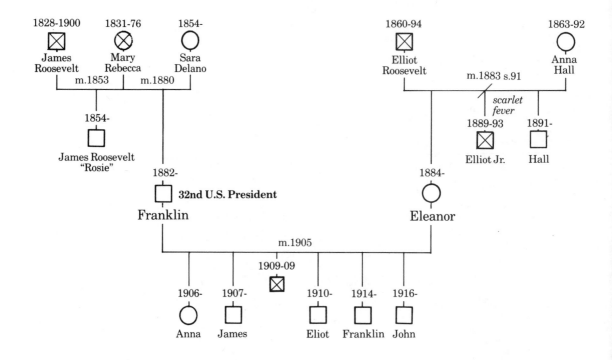

Diagram 3.11 Eleanor and Franklin Roosevelt

When two oldest children marry each other, they may have difficulty due to the lack of complementarity in their expected roles. Both may compete for power in the relationship. The Roosevelts (Diagram 3.11) are an example of a strong-willed oldest (Eleanor) and an only child (Franklin) marrying each other. Their marriage was reportedly a difficult one with conflicts around in-laws, careers, affairs and children. Their relationship became more complementary when Franklin was paralyzed by polio and Eleanor began to play a more critical role in his political career.

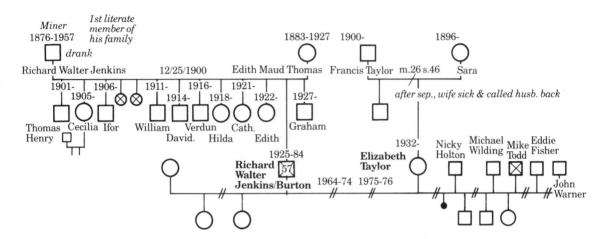

Diagram 3.12 Burton/Taylor – marriage of two younger siblings

On other hand, if two youngest children marry each other, they
may compete for "juniority" in the relationship, both waiting to be
taken care of. Richard Burton and Elizabeth Taylor, who married
and divorced each other twice, would be an example (Diagram 3.12)
of a younger marrying a younger. Burton was the second youngest
of thirteen children, but raised apart from his youngest brother.
Often in very large families a few of the younger children will have
the characteristics of a youngest. Taylor was the younger of two,
with an older brother whose needs were often sacrificed to her star-
dom, which, of course, compounded the tendencies of her sibling position as the "baby."

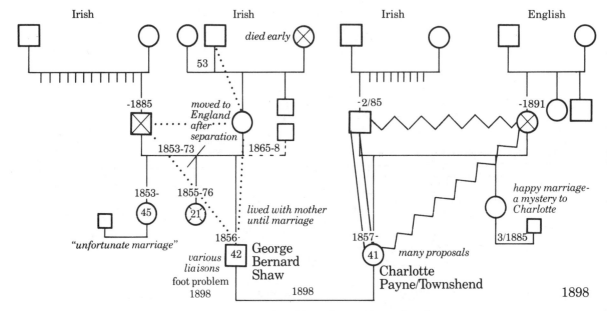

Diagram 3.13 Shaw/Payne-Townshend

When an oldest marries a youngest, there is a complementarity between the two sibling positions. This was the case of George Bernard Shaw (Diagram 3.13). He married an oldest (who was also the daughter of two oldests), who would take care of him and compensate for his slovenly ways. Charlotte married George possibly because she enjoyed his irreverence, creativity or irresponsibility, but certainly to have someone to take care of. They married at a time when George had become incapacitated with a foot problem, and Charlotte convinced him that if he didn't get care from her he would become a permanent invalid. In addition, George took advantage of Charlotte's wealth to support his mother, with whom he had lived until then. Although they later had many difficulties, the marriage lasted for 45 years, until Charlotte's death. Shaw once said that he could never have married anyone else, and the two of them, in a joint letter written only a few years before Charlotte's death, wrote: "Finally a marriage consolidates itself until the two lose all sense of separateness, and the married life becomes one life" (Dunbar, 1963, p. 286). There had been, in fact, much separateness between them, but still, the complementarity of their sibling positions and personalities was probably an important factor in their long-lived relationship.

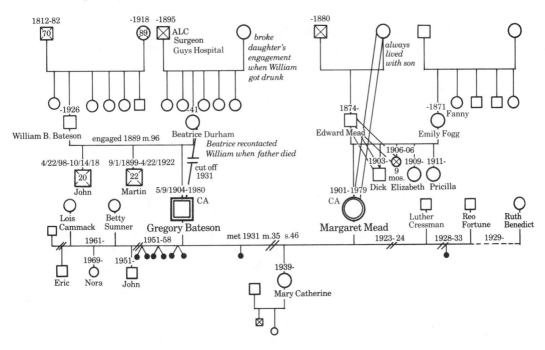

Diagram 3.14 Bateson/Mead

Of course, spouses from complementary sibling constellations may have problems, in which case it may be important to check the particular family more closely. A case in point is that of Margaret Mead, an oldest, and Gregory Bateson, a youngest (Diagram 3.14). Their sibling positions seem clearly reflected in their personality styles. As their daughter, Catherine describes it:

> Margaret's approach must have been based on early success in dealing with problems, perhaps related to the experience of being an older child and amplified by years of successfully organizing the younger ones. Gregory's experience was that of a younger child with relatively little capacity for changing what went on around him. Instead he would seek understanding. Indeed, he had a kind of abhorrence for the effort to solve problems, whether they were medical or political. (Bateson, 1984, p. 176)

Mead's and Bateson's respective sibling positions and problem-solving styles did not lead, however, to a complementary helper-helped relationship, but to struggle and disappointment in the other. Margaret's role as the senior partner was emphasized by the fact that she was three years older than Gregory, as her mother, also an oldest, was three years older than her husband. Their daughter describes their relationship:

> In the marriage she was the one who set the patterns, for Gregory lacked this fascination with pervasive elaboration. . . . His life was full of loose ends and unstitched edges, while for Margaret each thread became an occasion for embroidery. (p. 27)

> It was Gregory, more than anyone else, who lashed back at her for trying to manage his life. . . . She would see a problem and her imagination would leap to a solution. (p. 111)

> (He) began with his rebellion against Margaret, a rebellion shot through with resentment against his family and especially against his mother. (p. 160)

> It may well be that the suicide of his brother Martin in 1922, which followed on heavy-handed parental attempts at guidance and led to a period of increasing efforts to shape Gregory's choices as well, was an ingredient in his anxiety about problem solving and indeed about any effort to act in the world. (p. 176)

This description of Bateson reflects well his position as a youngest, waiting to be taken care of, yet rebellious against the one (Margaret, an oldest) who does it. In a sense, Gregory was a youngest who became an oldest due to the death of his brothers but who could never accept that definition of himself. The expectations of his sibling position were changed by the traumatic deaths of his two older brothers, thrusting him at age 18 into the position of only child and replacement for the loss endured by his family. The shift in Gregory's sibling position in early adult life may thus have contributed to the incompatibility between him and Margaret, even though their birth positions were complementary.

There is some similarity between Gregory, whose role in his family as the only surviving child intensified to the point of toxicity his relationship with his mother, and Margaret Mead's father, who was an only child doted on by his mother after his father's death when he was only six. While Bateson cut off from his mother, Edward Mead brought his mother with him into his marriage and she lived in the Mead household for the rest of her life.

Not surprisingly, middle children may show characteristics of either the oldest or the youngest, or both combined. Frequently a middle child, unless he or she is the only girl or only boy, has to struggle for a role in the family. Such a child may escape certain intensities directed at the oldest or the youngest, but this child may also have to struggle to be noticed.

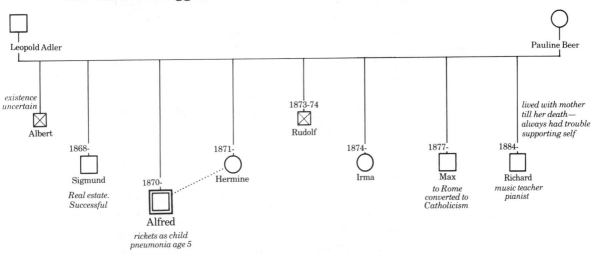

Diagram 3.15 Adler genogram

Alfred Adler (Diagram 3.15) is a good example of a middle child. Adler was one of the first to theorize about the importance of sibling constellation for family development, and it is clear many of his ideas derived from his personal experience. Ellenberger, a historian of psychiatry, describes Adler's ideas as follows:

> According to Adler, each one of the children in a family is born and grows up with a specific perspective according to its position in relation to the other siblings. From the outset the position of the oldest brother is better than that of the younger ones. He is made to feel that he is the stronger, the wiser, the most responsible. That is why he values the concept of authority and tradition and is conservative in his views. The youngest brother, on the other hand, is always in danger of remaining the spoiled and cowardly family baby. Whereas the oldest will take his father's profession, the youngest may easily become an artist, or then, as the result of overcompensation, he will develop tremendous ambition and strive to be the savior of the entire

family. The second child in a family is under perpetual pressure from both sides, striving to outmatch his older brother and fearing to be overtaken by the younger one. As for the only child, he is even more exposed to be spoiled and pampered than the youngest one. His parents' preoccupation with his health may cause him to become anxious and timorous. Such patterns are subject to modifications according to the distance between siblings and according to the proportion of boys and girls and their respective position in the family. If the oldest brother is closely followed by a sister, there comes a time when he will fear being outdistanced by the girl who will mature more rapidly than he. Among many other possible situations are those of the only girl in a family of boys, and of the only boy among a constellation of girls (a particularly unfavorable situation according to Adler). (1970, pp. 613–14)

This appears to fit with Adler's own family experience. Adler, who himself was sickly as a child (he had rickets, nearly died of pneumonia at age five, and was twice hit by moving vehicles), felt he grew up in the shadow of his older brother, Sigmund, who became a successful businessman, following in his father's footsteps. As can be seen on the genogram, Alfred was followed closely by his sister, Hermine, with whom he apparently had little relationship in adulthood. The next brother died in bed next to Alfred when the latter was four. The next brother, Max, who was apparently very envious of Adler, distanced from the family by moving to Rome and converting to Catholicism, and the youngest brother, Richard, seems indeed to have been spoiled. He lived with his mother until her death and, although he saw himself as an artist and musician, always had trouble supporting himself, living at times with Adler's family and receiving support from Adler.

Missing information is immediately apparent on a genogram. In Adler's case, in spite of his explicit belief about the importance of sibling relationships in determining behavior, most of his biographers have given only sketchy and conflicting information about his own sibling constellation (Bottome, 1939; Furtmuller, 1979; Orgler, 1963; Sperber, 1974). We know even less about the sibling or family patterns of Adler's parents, a fact which is true also for Freud, Horney, and Jung, in spite of the great interest there has been in their work and their psychological makeup. Clearly, biographers have yet to take a systemic view of history.

Siblings' Gender

Gender is another important factor in interpreting sibling constellation patterns on a genogram. The hypothesis here is that a person's siblings provide a model for his or her experiences with peers. Thus, someone with all sisters will have had a great deal of experience with girls but little experience with boys and vice versa.

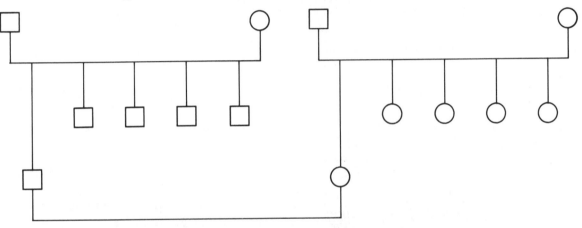

Diagram 3.16 Marriage of two oldest from same-sexed system

Such experiences (or lack thereof) with the opposite sex may also affect marital compatibility, as in Diagram 3.16. Both spouses in this genogram have had experiences only with siblings of their own sex. The husband who comes from an all-male sibling constellation will probably perceive women as "other" and will have to work harder to understand his wife than a male who has had a sister would. Similarly, the wife who comes from an all-female sibling constellation will probably have had more peer experience with women and less with men. In addition, such gender-related sibling experiences intersect with birth order to make this couple particularly noncomplementary. Each is an oldest and thus has had experience dealing with younger siblings. Seeing this pattern on the genogram, one would predict a good deal of difficulty in initial adjustment after marriage.

Distance in Age Between Siblings

Another factor in understanding family constellations is the distance in age between siblings. A rule of thumb is that the closer siblings are in age, the more they have shared in life experience, identical twins exemplifying the most extreme case of sharing. The further apart they are in age, the less sibling experience they have probably had. In general, siblings who are more than six years apart are more like only children than like siblings, since they have gone through each phase of development separately.

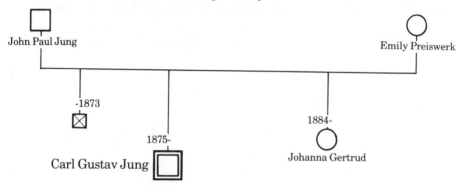

Diagram 3.17 Jung as an only child

Jung (Diagram 3.17) is an example of a functional only child due to this factor. Since his older brother died before he was born and his sister was born nine years later, Jung's experience would be more like that of an only child than of a sibling.

Often, in large sibling systems, there is a breakdown according to sex and distance in age, so that, for example, two brothers born 18 months apart may form a dyad and their two younger sisters born five and seven years later form a second subsystem, as in Diagram 3.18. (We have used parentheses to indicate the subsystems.)

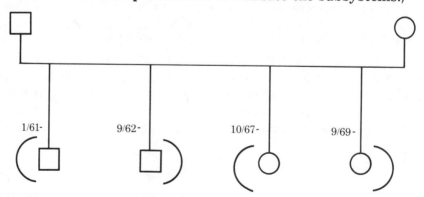

Diagram 3.18 Sibling constellation showing subsystems

Other Factors Influencing Sibling Constellation

It is important not to take the hypotheses about sibling constellations too literally. Many people fit the characterizations, but many do not. Also, the usual sibling constellation predictions may be influenced by a number of other factors.

In fact, the empirical research on sibling constellations is at best inconclusive, because there are so many other factors that can change or moderate the influence of sibling constellation. Nevertheless, an awareness of sibling constellation can provide clinically useful normalizing explanations of people's roles in their family, as well as indicating other factors to explore when the typical patterns are not found. In addition, adult siblings, often ignored by family therapists, can, depending on their sibling constellation, be extremely important resources in therapy.

For example, Sigmund Freud in many ways functioned as an only child. He seemed to have had a special position in his family beyond just being the oldest. In fact, Freud never once in his autobiography refers to any of his siblings, although there were seven children born in close succession following his birth and, except for the one who died, they all grew up with Sigmund (Diagram 3.19).

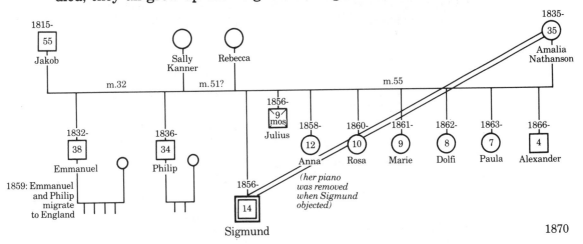

Diagram 3.19 Freud – functional only

Although older siblings are generally less aware of younger siblings than vice versa, the degree of Sigmund Freud's "specialness" in his family might lead one to consider other factors. Perhaps his tendency to view himself as an only reflected his mother's strong preference for him over his siblings (as evidenced, for example, by her removing Anna's piano when he objected to the music). But why would this be so? One factor may have been that Sigmund as the first child was the fulfillment of his mother's wish for her own family with Jacob, who had been married twice before and already had sons her own age. For Jakob, Sigmund may have been a replacement for his two oldest sons who had left both home and country. Another factor may have been the loss of a second son a year after Sigmund's birth and then a long succession of girls, making Sigmund's position as the only son (until Alexander's birth 10 years later) even more special. Of course, there may have been other factors as well. Unfortunately, we know almost nothing about Sigmund's mother's family of origin. Perhaps he reminded her of someone else or was a replacement for someone she lost.

As Freud's family illustrates, there are many factors that may influence the role of sibling constellation, some of which are discussed below.

The timing of each sibling's birth in the family's history: Sometimes, when a child is born at a critical point in a family history, there are special expectations for that child, in addition to those typical of his or her sibling position. These expectations may exaggerate a sibling position characterization (as with the oldest who acts super-responsible) or modify the usual sibling roles (as with a middle or youngest who functions as an oldest or only child). Particularly critical are family deaths and transitions. Here, critical family life events (Category 4) intersect with family structure (Category 1). For example, a child born around the time one of the grandparents dies may play a special role in the family (Mueller & McGoldrick Orfanidis, 1976; Walsh, 1978). With this factor in mind, we notice that Freud was born not only at the start of a remarried family, but also within a few months of the death of his paternal grandfather (p. 20). We will discuss the impact of critical events in more detail under Category 4.

The child's characteristics: A child with special characteristics may also shift the expected sibling patterns in a family. For example, a second child may become the functional oldest if he or she is particularly talented or if the oldest is sickly. Or an older child may be treated as a youngest if he or she has special problems (e.g., asthma, truancy, misbehavior, phobias, etc.). Clinicians often see this phenomenon in child-focused families. It is important for the clinician to include such relevant information when it is known.

The family's "program" for the child: For reasons that are not always clear, families may have a specific set of expectations for a particular child, seemingly independent of where he or she fits in the family constellation. Naming patterns of siblings are often significant signals of family "programming." For example, Gregory Bateson, named for one of his father's heroes, Gregor Mendel, was perhaps being "programmed" to aim at great accomplishments as a natural scientist. On the other hand, John Quincy Adams broke the family tradition of naming the oldest son John to name his first son George Washington Adams, after his father's greatly disliked political rival (see pp. 48 and 78 for further discussion).

Although names or nicknames may give hints on the genogram as to the family's "programming," the clinician needs to look for other indications. For example, an examination of the Kennedy family's history (Diagram 3.36, p. 89) suggests that the males were programmed to run for office. As is well-known, the oldest son of Joseph P. Kennedy was slated by his father to run for president, but died before he could. His three brothers all later did run for president and two of his brothers-in-law ran for vice-president or governor. Not surprisingly, a number of the grandsons have also become involved in politics.

Parental attitudes and biases regarding sex differences: Parents' attitudes and beliefs about gender roles influence their expectations for their different children in profound ways. For example, families in most cultures have always shown a preference for sons. This means that an older brother who has a younger sister will tend to be in a more favored position than an older sister who has a younger brother. In the latter case, the sister will often have the responsibilities of an oldest, while her younger brother will get the glory and high expectations. Examples of younger brothers of older sisters who became functional oldests would be Thomas Jefferson (see p.

68), John Quincy Adams (see p. 78), and Martin Luther King, Jr. (Diagram 3.20).

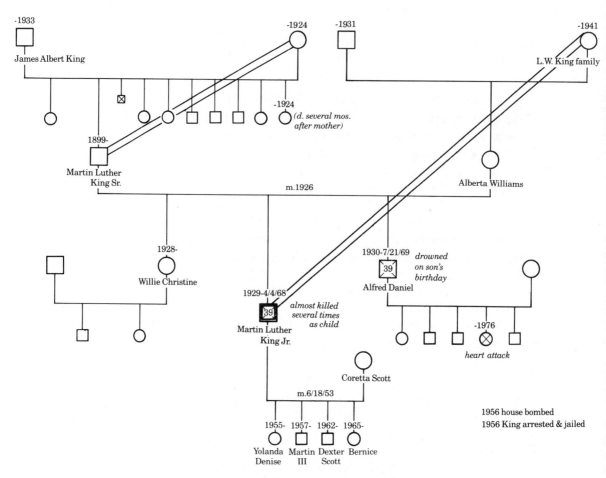

Diagram 3.20 King – functional oldest

It is interesting that in the Hennig study (Hennig & Jardim, 1977) of highly successful women in business, not a single woman in the sample of 25 had a brother. Recent research indicates that while the preference for sons is diminishing (Entwistle & Doering, 1981), there is still a greater likelihood that a family with only female children will continue to try for another, while families with only sons will stop with fewer children (Broverman et al., 1972).

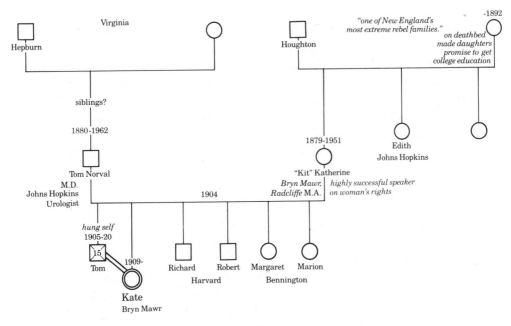

Diagram 3.21 Hepburn

Katharine Hepburn (Diagram 3.21) appears to have become a functional oldest after her older brother hung himself at the age of 15, when she was 11. As a functional oldest, she was a conscientious achiever and her parents had high expectations for her. Several other factors may have influenced this, including the fact that her maternal grandmother cared so much about the advancement of women that she elicited from her three daughters a deathbed promise that they would all go to college. Hepburn's mother, the oldest, was herself a highly successful speaker on women's rights.

As already mentioned, the Kennedy family had high expectations of sons. One factor that may have influenced this was that Joseph Kennedy, the father, was the oldest and only son of a youngest and only surviving son (P.J.), whose own father, Patrick, died at age 35 the year P.J. was born. A paternal granduncle, John Kennedy, died at one year of age in 1855 (see p. 89). The multitude of male deaths (even up to the present) may have intensified the importance of males in this family.

As parental attitudes and biases about gender change, one would expect that the role of gender in understanding sibling constellation will change as well.

The child's sibling position in relation to that of the parent: The child's position in the family may be particularly highlighted if it repeats the position of the same-sexed parent. Thus, a man who is the oldest son of an oldest son (as in the case of John Quincy Adams — see p. 78) may have certain specific expectations placed on him that do not apply to his younger brother. If a man's relationship with his own father was charged, there is a good chance that in the next generation the relationship with his son in the same ordinal position may also turn sour. (We will discuss this issue further under Category 3, Pattern Repetition.)

Unusual Family Configurations

In scanning the genogram, sometimes certain structural configurations will "jump out" at the clinician, suggesting critical family themes or problems. A good example of this is the complex genogram of the Fonda family presented in Chapter 2 (p. 24). What is immediately apparent from the genogram structure is the multitude of remarriages in this family. Such a configuration should cue the clinician to the likely importance of the theme of divorce and remarriage in this family.

At least three aspects of the graphic structural configuration are striking in examining the genogram of Elizabeth Blackwell, the first U.S. woman physician (Diagram 3.22): first, the preponderance of successful professional women; second, the fact that none of Samuel Blackwell's five sisters ever married, nor did any of his five daughters and only a few of the 14 women in the third generation; and third, the frequency of their adopting children.

This configuration opens up for further exploration the role of gender in this family of extraordinarily successful women. It would be fascinating to know the rules and attitudes in the family that influenced such a pattern. Some of these have been suggested by Horn (1983), who says that the family viewed marriage negatively and actively discouraged the daughters from marrying. One very interesting fact is that two of Elizabeth's three sisters-in-law, Lucy Stone, the famous suffragette, and Antoinette Brown, the first woman minister in the U.S., who had become best friends in college at Oberlin, had resolved between themselves, long before meeting the Blackwell family, never to marry but to adopt and raise children! It is also interesting that of the five Blackwell sisters, four were very successful

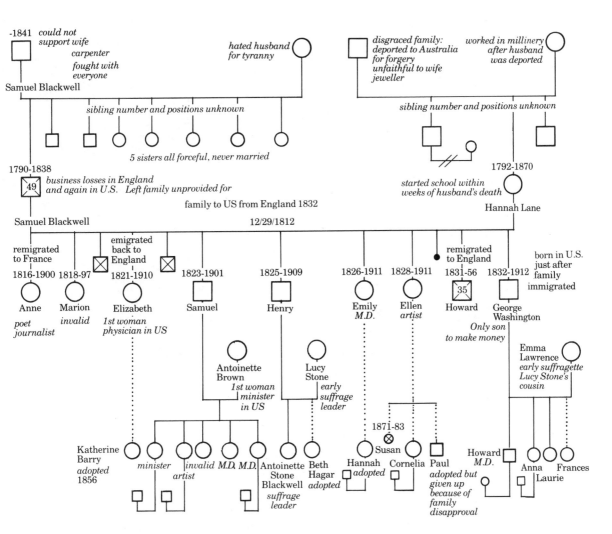

Diagram 3.22 Blackwell

(Elizabeth and Emily as physicians, Anna as a writer, and Ellen as
an artist), and the fifth was an invalid. Of the five daughters of their
brother Samuel, two also became physicians, two became ministers,
and the fifth was also an invalid.

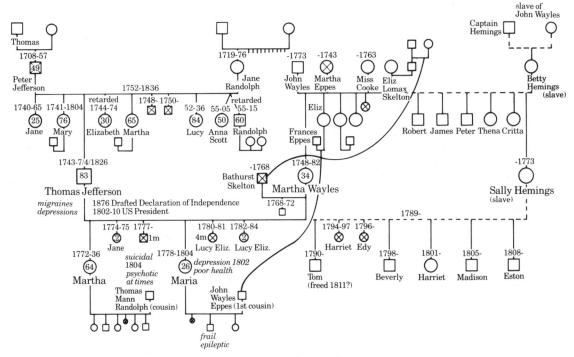

Diagram 3.23 Jefferson

Possibly one of the most convoluted family genograms we have ever attempted is that of Thomas Jefferson, the third President of the United States (Diagram 3.23). Making sense of this unusual configuration is a challenge. There are many interconnected affairs and relationships in the family. Jefferson's father-in-law had a long relationship with Betty Hemings, by whom he had six children, and Jefferson later had a long relationship and seven children with Betty's daughter, Sally Hemings. Furthermore, Jefferson's daughters both married relatives; Martha married a cousin on her paternal grandmother's side, and Maria married her maternal first cousin. In addition, Martha Jefferson's first husband was the younger brother of her second stepmother's first husband. To say this family is a "too richly cross-joined system" (Hoffman, 1981) is an understatement.

Another example of an unusual family configuration would be a family in which two siblings married siblings from another family, such as the Freud/Bernays family (see p. 27).

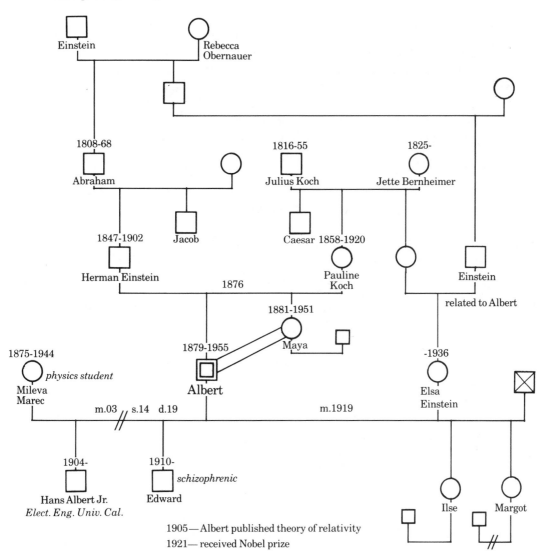

Diagram 3.24 Einstein

And then there is Albert Einstein, who left his first wife to marry a woman who was his first cousin on his mother's side and his second cousin on his father's side (Diagram 3.24).

The unusual connections seen in the graphic configurations of the Jefferson, Freud/Bernays, and Einstein families might lead to a number of speculations about triangles set up by these intrafamily marriages (see Category 5, Relational Patterns and Triangles), as well as about possible family expectations influencing members against marrying outside the group. In Jefferson's case, for example, we know that his wife elicited from him a deathbed promise that he would not remarry, and he himself, having lost his wife and four children, was protective with his two daughters and apparently encouraged them, as well as many of his slaves, to marry within the family (Brodie, 1974, p. 47). In terms of relationships, we know that Jefferson was extremely close to his daughter Martha. Perhaps not surprisingly, he had many problems relating to her husband, Thomas Mann Randolph, and felt closer to his other son-in-law, John Wayles Eppes, the son of his wife's sister, Elizabeth. Randolph, in fact, became very jealous of Eppes, sensing Jefferson's preference for the latter.

Unusual family configurations on the genogram should also cue the clinician to the application of other interpretive principles. Thus, repeating graphic patterns (e.g., multiple remarriages in each generation) might suggest pattern repetition across generations (Category 3), while structural contrasts (e.g., one spouse coming from a large family and the other an only child) might suggest family imbalance (Category 6).

In summary, one can come up with numerous hypotheses simply by examining the relational structure, including family composition, sibling constellations, and unusual family configurations. By examining the family structure alone one can hypothesize about certain themes, roles, and relationships which may then be checked out by eliciting further information about the family.

CATEGORY 2: LIFE CYCLE FIT

The second category involves an understanding of the life cycle transitions a family is adapting to. The fit of ages and dates on a genogram allows one to see whether life cycle events occur within normative expectations. When they do not, possible difficulties in managing that phase of the family life cycle can be further explored. A family progresses through a series of milestones, transitions, or nodal points in its development, including leaving home, marriage, the birth of children, child-rearing, launching, retirement, etc. At each nodal point in the life cycle the family must reorganize itself in order to move on successfully to the next phase. These transitions can be very difficult for some families, whose patterns rigidify at transition points, and who have trouble adapting to new circumstances. (For an extensive discussion of the family life cycle, see Carter & McGoldrick, 1980.) It is important to track symptoms in relation to a family's mastery of the tasks for their particular life cycle stage.

There are normative expectations for the timing of each phase of the family life cycle, i.e., the likely ages of family members at each transition point. While these norms are ever-changing and must not be regarded in any way as fixed, when events happen outside this range of expectations, the clinician should consider the possibility of some difficulty inhibiting the family in making the life cycle transition.

Thus, it is important to scan the genogram for family members whose ages differ greatly from the norm for their phase of the life cycle. The dates on the genogram of births, deaths, leaving home, marriage, separation, and divorce are all helpful in this regard. For example, the fact that three sons in a family married for the first time in their fifties might indicate some problems in leaving home and forming intimate relationships. It would be worth asking a couple in which the husband is 27 and the wife 47 how they happened to get together and how this pairing might be a fit with various patterns from their families of origin. A woman who has her first child at 43, a man who becomes a father at age 70, or a family in which all the sons died before middle age – all suggest systems where deviations in the normative pattern of the life cycle deserve further exploration.

For example, George Bernard Shaw and his wife, Charlotte Payne-Townshend, married in their early forties (see p. 54), leading us to wonder about their hesitations regarding marriage. Both of them had, in fact, experienced very unhappy childhoods as a result of their parents' unhappy marriages and were at best ambivalent about intimacy.

In our culture, there appears to be a generally preferable time in the life cycle for couples to marry (see McGoldrick, 1980). Recently, the norms for marriage have been changing; couples are marrying later, often in their mid-twenties or later. Statistically, couples who marry before the age of 20 or after the age of 30 are at greater risk for divorce (Booth & Edwards, 1985). It is clear that marital cooperation was quite a task for the Shaws, both of whom were set in their ways by the time of their marriage.

Also of interest is the period of time between meeting, engagement, and marriage, and between separation, divorce, and remarriage. Generally, we believe that a short interval between marriages does not allow time for family members to deal with the emotional shifts involved (McGoldrick & Carter, 1980). For example, Henry Fonda remarried very quickly, eight months after his second wife committed suicide (see p. 24). Such an observation on a genogram suggests unresolved emotional issues and at least the possibility of an affair. In fact, Henry had begun an affair with his future wife the year before. Rushing into the new marriage also suggests the importance to Henry of putting the previous marriage behind him. One would also wonder how the family, particularly the children, adjusted to such rapid family changes. In light of this, the fact that Peter shot himself in the stomach while his father was on his third honeymoon becomes more understandable.

Gregory Bateson's parents are an example of a couple who had a prolonged courtship (see p. 84). Seeing this on the genogram should lead one to inquire further about possible difficulties in the courtship. As it turns out, Beatrice's mother called off her daughter's engagement when William Bateson got drunk – her husband was an alcoholic – and Beatrice recontacted William through an ad shortly after her father died and married him soon afterwards.

Sometimes, a family will have difficulty with the launching phase, in which their children leave home. The children have difficulty starting their own families and may stay with their parents all their lives. An example would be the Bronte family. The genogram (Diagram 3.25) shows that all the Bronte children had difficulty leaving home and all died before the age of 40. Only Charlotte managed to marry, at the late age of 38. She died nine months later, a few months after becoming pregnant and just after her childhood nurse died. Such a genogram would raise questions about the early programming of the children in this family. In fact, as is evident from the genogram, all six children were born in a seven-year period and their mother became fatally ill with cancer shortly after the birth of the young-

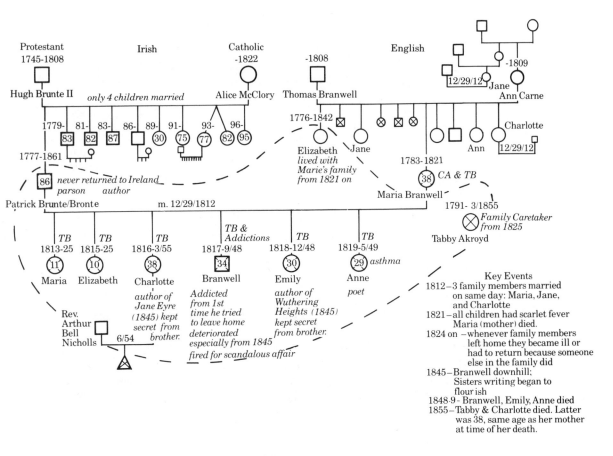

Diagram 3.25 Bronte sisters

est. After she died, the children were raised in virtual isolation, never seeing other children. Nothing was changed or painted in the home for the next 30 years. The children turned inward to their imagination and to each other, developing a private shared fantasy life. From childhood onwards, over a period of many years, they together wrote many hundreds of manuscripts in their own hardly decipherable language. In adulthood all three sisters became accomplished writers. However, whenever any of them tried to leave home they suffered a variety of symptoms and returned before long.

Also apparent on a genogram are life cycle discrepancies, e.g., when two people get married who are at very different points in their individual life cycles. An example of this would be the marriage of

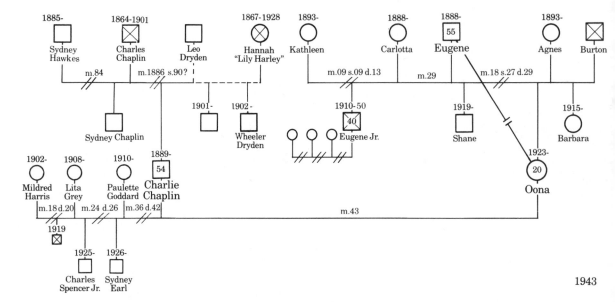

Diagram 3.26 Oona O'Neill and Chaplin at the time of their marriage

Oona O'Neill, the daughter of Eugene O'Neill, to Charlie Chaplin (Diagram 3.26). Chaplin was 30 years older than Oona, practically the age of her father. In addition, Chaplin had been married three times before, while Oona had not left home until the marriage. They married after a very brief courtship. Her father was enraged and remained estranged from Oona for the rest of his life. Despite this, their marriage was reportedly a successful one.

Finally, Sigmund Freud's father, Jakob, at age 40, married Amalia, who was only 20 (Diagram 3.27). His two sons were contemporaries of his wife, which could present a problem for a newlywed husband, as indeed seems to have been the case. Jakob soon arranged for his two oldest sons to emigrate to England, a safe distance, perhaps, from him and his young wife (Clark, 1980, p. 14).

> In sum, ages and dates on the genogram allow one to see what life cycle transitions the family is adapting to and whether life cycle events and ages occur within normative expectations. When they do not, possible difficulties in managing that phase of the life cycle can be further explored.

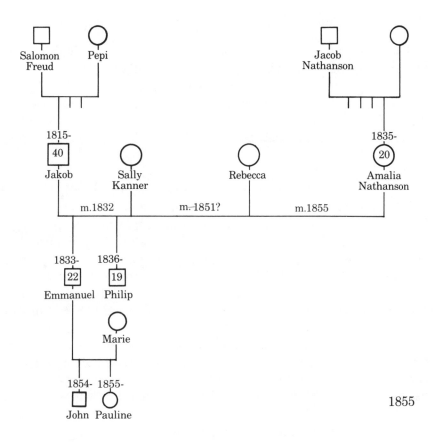

Diagram 3.27 Freud family at time of third marriage

CATEGORY 3: PATTERN REPETITION
ACROSS GENERATIONS

Since family patterns can be transmitted from one generation to the next, the clinician should scan the genogram for patterns that have repeated over several generations. Such repetitive patterns occur in functioning, relationship, and family structure. Recognizing such patterns can often help families avoid repeating unfortunate patterns in the present and transmitting them into the future.

Patterns of Functioning

The functioning of family members may repeat itself across several generations. In such cases, a particular style of functioning (whether adaptive or maladaptive) or of dealing with problems is passed down from one generation to the next. This transmission does not necessarily occur in linear fashion. An alcoholic father may have children who become teetotalers, and their children may again become drinkers.

Often the presenting problem of the family will have occurred in previous generations. Numerous symptomatic patterns, such as alcoholism, incest, physical symptoms, violence, and suicide, tend to be repeated in families from generation to generation. By noting the pattern repetition, the clinician may be helped to understand the family's present adaptation to the situation and may suggest interventions to short-circuit the process. For example, let's look again at the Fonda genogram (see p. 24). It is clear that there is a repetition of suicidal behavior in this family. Peter Fonda shot himself in the stomach less than a year after his mother's suicide, and Margaret Sullavan's daughter Brigit committed suicide a year after her mother did the same. Given the evidence that one suicide seems to make suicide an option for others in the family (Cain, 1972; Rohrbaugh, McGoldrick, & Durks, 1985), specific efforts at suicide prevention may well be indicated in such families. The same can be said for preventive intervention in families with a history of such symptoms as alcohol abuse and incest.

The genogram of Eugene O'Neill, the famous playwright, is an example of alcohol and drug abuse seen across several generations (Diagram 3.28). Alcohol (as indicated by ALC) and drug abuse is shown in each generation, seeming to become more and more self-destructive. Also evident (and possibly related) is a pattern of marital instability. According to O'Neill and so successfully portrayed in his plays, his parents' relationship was a stormy and painful one. Eugene himself married three times and his oldest son, Eugene, Jr., followed this same pattern. The oldest sons died young in this family: Eugene's oldest brother drank himself to death by the age of 45, and his oldest son committed suicide at the age of 40.

O'Neill was quite aware of the power of the past to presage the future. In many of his plays he recreated his family of origin in an effort to exorcise its influence, but knew he was unsuccessful. In fact, in *Long Day's Journey Into Night* Mary (his mother) replies to Ty-

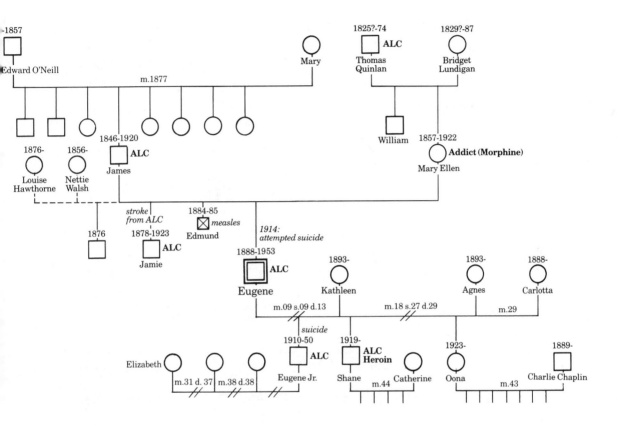

Diagram 3.28 O'Neill family – repetitive functioning patterns

rone (his father), when he urges her not to bring up the past, "How can I? The past is the present, isn't it? It's the future too. We all try to lie out of that, but life won't let us" (O'Neill, 1955, p. 87). Fortunately for us, Eugene O'Neill was able to make art out of this long family pattern of tragedy.

One can track multigenerational patterns of success as well as failure in a family. The Blackwell family genogram (p. 67) shows a pattern of strong and successful women. Included in this remarkable family were the first woman physician and the first woman minister in the U.S., as well as numerous other successful woman physicians, ministers, artists, and suffragettes.

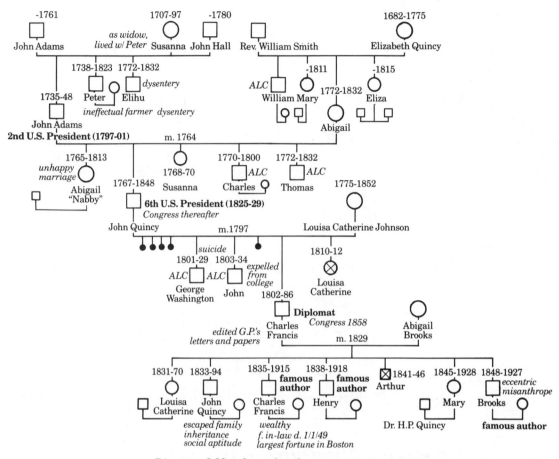

Diagram 3.29 Adams family — successes and failures

The Adams family (Diagram 3.29) also reveals a pattern of success over four generations. John Adams was the second President
of the United States. In the next generation, John Quincy Adams
repeated his father's performance as the sixth President of the United States. His son, Charles Francis Adams, was a famous diplomat
and statesman. And in the fourth generation, Charles Francis Jr.
and Henry Adams were both accomplished writers. However, one
biographer of the Adams Family, Nagel (1983), argues that such success did not come without a price. The Adams (as evidenced in their
letters) were severe, self-critical, and often melancholic, and the family members who were not so successful did quite poorly. Only in the
fifth generation were there no great successes and no great failures
either.

As seen in the Adams family, extreme success and failure may co-exist in the same family and in each succeeding generation. Again, we can refer to the Blackwell family (p. 67) where one daughter in each generation appears to have been an invalid while the others were quite successful. We will discuss this phenomenon again when we talk about balance and imbalance in families (Category 6).

Another common functioning pattern is success in one generation followed by remarkable failure in the next. This may be particularly true of the families of famous people, where children may feel pressure to live up to the reputations of their parents. For examples, see the genograms of the Kennedy (p. 89) and O'Neill families (p. 81).

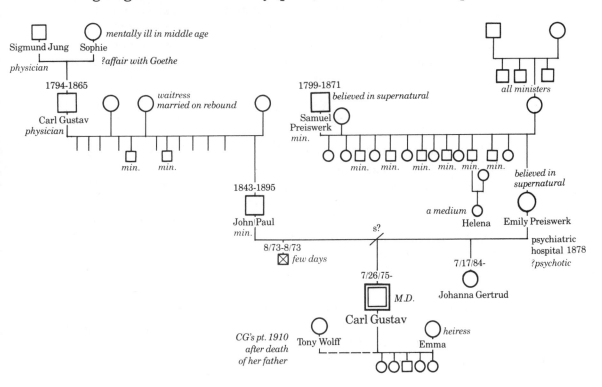

Diagram 3.30 Jung family

Specific patterns of functioning may also be repeated across the generations. A good example would be the genogram of Carl Gustav Jung (Diagram 3.30). A quick glance at his genogram shows the preponderance of ministers: Jung's father, two paternal uncles, all six

maternal uncles, the maternal grandfather and two maternal grand-
uncles. Next one sees that both his paternal grandfather, for whom
he was named, and his paternal great-grandfather were physicians,
and finally one can note several family members who believed in the
supernatural: his mother, maternal grandfather and maternal cousin,
Helena Preiswerk, who claimed to be a medium and whose seances
Jung attended in his youth. Thus, his becoming a physician with
a profound interest in religion and in the supernatural very much
fit with the predominant patterns in his family.

In a different vein would be the pattern of sexual activity across
the generations in the Kennedy family (see p. 89). The pattern of in-
numerable sexual exploits almost in plain view of their families was
characteristic of at least Joseph, his father-in-law, Honey Fitz, and
his first two sons, Joe Jr. and Jack. (Robert was extremely negative about this behavior.) We will discuss the Kennedy family in
more detail in a later section.

Patterns of Relationships

Relationship patterns of closeness, distance, conflict, etc., may
also repeat themselves over the generations. Some common relational patterns are discussed in a later section (Category 5). Here
we focus on their repetition across the generations. Genograms
often reveal complex relational patterns that would be missed if not
mapped across a few generations. Recognizing such patterns can,
it is hoped, help families avoid continuing the repetition in future
generations. One example of such a repetition would be a family in
which mother and son in each generation have a special alliance while
father and son have a negative conflictual relationship. Realizing
the predictability of such a pattern and the multigenerational programming involved, a son might choose consciously to change his
relationship with his parents to vary this pattern.

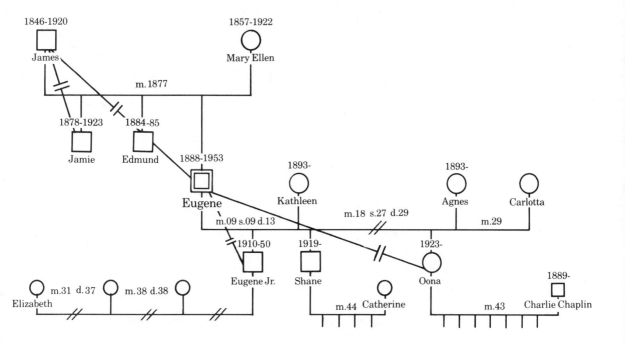

Diagram 3.31 O'Neill family – repetitive relationships

The O'Neill family (Diagram 3.31) shows a multigenerational pattern of estrangement between father and children. Both Eugene and his older brother Jamie felt estranged from their father, and all of them blamed each other for the mother's drug addiction. In the next generation, the playwright was totally estranged from his oldest son and had nothing to do with his daughter Oona after she married Charlie Chaplin.

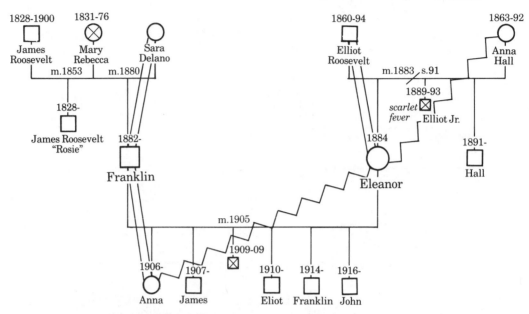

Diagram 3.32 Roosevelt family — repetitive relationships

In the family of Eleanor Roosevelt, the pattern was one of mother-daughter resentment and close feelings between father and daughter (Diagram 3.32). Although both her parents had died by the time she was 11, Eleanor remembered having a special relationship with her father while feeling her mother was harsh and insensitive to his predicament. Her father was in fact an alcoholic and quite irresponsible, and her mother had once committed him to an asylum and later separated from him. In the next generation, the daughter, Anna, an oldest like Eleanor, preferred her father and saw her own mother as overly harsh. Throughout her adolescence she had a stormy relationship with Eleanor, which did not change until her father contracted polio.

Repeated Structural Patterns

It is common for family patterns to intensify when there is a repetition of structure from one generation to another. In particular, people in a similar structural pattern as the previous generation are likely to repeat the patterns of that generation. Thus, as we look for a repetition of functioning and relationships, we also look for a repetition of family structure.

For example, a mother who is the youngest of three sisters will probably find herself overidentifying with her youngest if she also has three daughters. Or, if one comes from a family of three generations of separation and divorce, one's expectations may be that divorce is almost a norm.

We have already mentioned that George Bernard Shaw was the youngest son of a youngest son (p. 54). John Quincy Adams, on the other hand, was the oldest son of an oldest son (p. 78). Such repetitive structural patterns should cue the clinician to a possible overidentification of parent with child and an intensification of cross-generational patterns.

To summarize the principle for interpreting pattern repetition across generations, repetitive patterns of functioning, relationship, and family structure on a genogram suggest the possibility of the patterns continuing in the present and into the future. Recognition of these patterns offers the possibility of helping family members alter these patterns.

CATEGORY 4: LIFE EVENTS AND FAMILY FUNCTIONING

Category 4 involves understanding how life events and changes in family functioning are interconnected. Since the genogram records many critical dates in the family's history, it is useful to the clinician for looking at coincidences of various life events and changes in family functioning. Often seemingly unconnected events that occur around the same time in a family's history are systematically related and have a profound impact on family functioning.

It is particularly helpful to track changes in a family's long-term functioning as they relate to critical family life events. We examine the genogram carefully for a pile-up of stresses, the impact of traumatic events, anniversary reactions, and the relationship of family experiences to social, economic and political events. Thus, we can assess the impact of change on the family and its vulnerability to future changes.

The Coincidences of Life Events

Any time that several critical family experiences occur around the
same time, it is wise to request details. These may lead to connections which help unravel important emotional and systemic patterns.
Such "coincidences" may indicate a stressful period in the family's
history. We are not talking here about one event "causing" another,
but about the association of events which may be influential in the
development of family patterns. For example, on Gregory Bateson's
genogram (Diagram 3.33), one can observe a number of interesting
coincidences.

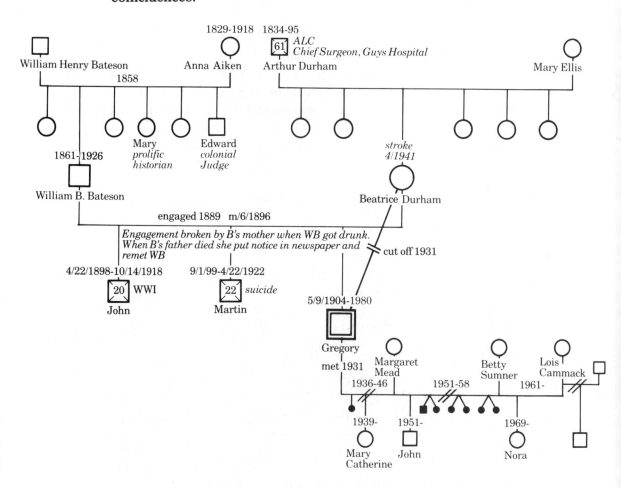

Diagram 3.33 Bateson family

First of all, Gregory's parents were married shortly after the death of his mother's father. Secondly, Martin committed suicide on his brother John's birthday, four years after John died. And finally, Gregory met Margaret Mead shortly after he cut off from his mother.

Viewed systemically, these events may be more than coincidence. As mentioned earlier, Gregory's parents' engagement was called off by Beatrice's mother when W. B. Bateson got drunk. This was a reaction to Beatrice's father's alcoholism. However, three months after the alcoholic father died, Beatrice put a notice in the newspaper, hoping to reconnect with W.B., and they remet and were married shortly afterward. In the next generation, Gregory happened to meet and fall in love with Margaret just after becoming estranged from his mother. She and her second husband were doing anthropological work in a remote area of the world at that time. One might speculate that the children in this family could only connect to their spouses after disconnecting, through death or cut-off, from a parent.

Gregory Bateson was the youngest of three sons of a famous British geneticist. Gregory was considered the least promising of the three, sickly in childhood and not an outstanding student. The oldest son, John, was supposed to be the leader. He and the middle brother, Martin, two years apart in age, were extremely close. Gregory was four years younger and grew up somewhat separately. When John was 20 he was killed in World War I. A few days later his mother wrote to Martin that " . . . you and Gregory are left to me still and you must help me back to some of the braveness that John has taken away" (Lipset, 1980, p. 71).

Following John's death a rift developed between Martin and his father. William Bateson's mother had died two months before John (another coincidence), and William now began to pressure his second son, who was a poet, to become a zoologist. Relations between father and son deteriorated. When, in addition, Martin felt rebuffed by a young woman he admired, he took a gun and shot himself in Trafalgar Square on his brother John's birthday, April 22, 1922, in what was described as "probably the most dramatic and deliberate suicide ever witnessed in London" (Lipset, 1980, p. 93). Martin's choosing to kill himself on his brother's birthday is also an example of an anniversary reaction, which will be discussed in a later section.

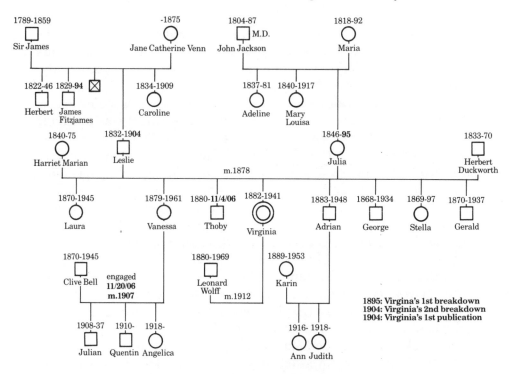

Diagram 3.34 Virginia Woolf—coincidences

The genogram of Virginia Woolf (Diagram 3.34) provides another example of the interconnectedness of events. Virginia's first two "mental breakdowns" at the ages of 13 and 22 (both of which possibly involved suicide attempts) occurred shortly after the deaths of her mother in 1895 and her father in 1904. After recovering from her second breakdown, Virginia wrote and published her first article, still in the same year as her father's death. As her biographer puts it, "Virginia felt she ought to earn some money, if only to recoup some of the expenses of her illness . . . " (Bell, 1972, p. 93), but we might also speculate that the death of her father (a renowned writer himself) in some way freed her to publish. Also of interest, her older sister, Vanessa, became engaged two weeks after her brother's death. Again, such "coincidences" might be the starting point for further exploration.

Sometimes, as in the Freud family, there were certain critical periods during which a number of important family events occurred. A careful examination of the Freud genogram in Diagram 3.35 reveals two such periods. The first period occurred around Sigmund's

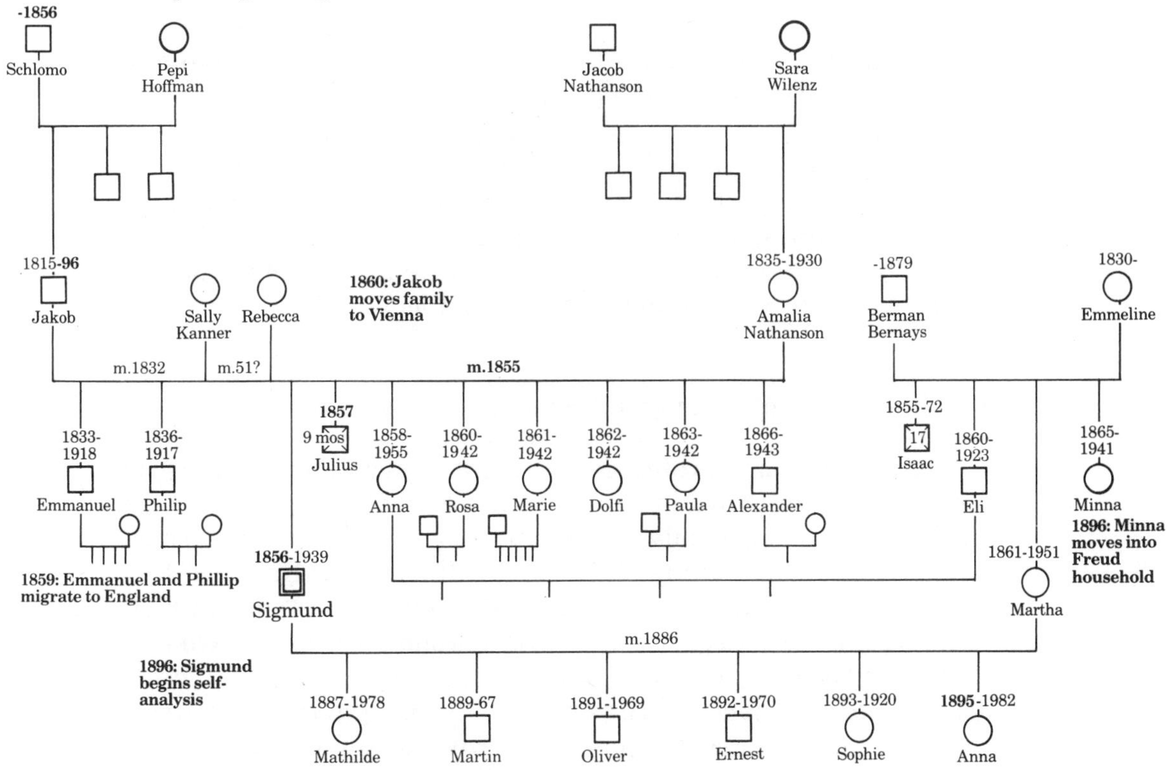

Diagram 3.35 Freud – critical periods and coincidences

birth. In 1855, his father, Jakob, married his mother, Amalia. Seven months later, Jakob's father died. Three months after this, Sigmund, the family favorite, was born. A year later, Julius was born, but he only lived for eight months. Two years later, Jakob's oldest sons emigrated to England. A year after that, Jakob moved the whole family to Vienna. A second critical period occurred from 1895 to 1896. Freud's favorite child, Anna, was born on December 3, 1895. The following year Freud's sister-in-law, Minna, moved into the household, and on December 23 of that year Sigmund's father died, a loss that Sigmund considered the most significant and upsetting in the life of a man. Perhaps it is not surprising that he published his first analytic paper ("Studies on Hysteria") and began his famous self-analysis during this period as well.

Interestingly, both critical periods occurred at transitional points in the Freud family life cycle. The first occurred around a marriage (Jakob's third) and the second around the birth of the last child. In clinical practice, we have found that families are more vulnerable to change (including dysfunction) around transitional points in the family life cycle. Thus, we pay particular attention to these nodal points in examining genograms for coincidences of family events and/or changes in family functioning.

In sum, it is important to notice the coinciding dates on the genogram. Sometimes, interesting systemic connections can be found. If nothing else, they pinpoint the critical periods in a family history, which are likely to have left an emotional legacy.

The Impact of Life Changes, Transitions, and Traumas

Critical life changes, transitions, and traumas can have a dramatic impact on a family system and its members. Our own experience has led us to pay particular attention to the impact of losses, since families are much more likely to have difficulty readjusting after a loss than after other family changes (McGoldrick & Walsh, 1983).

We have already seen the impact that John Bateson's death had on Martin Bateson, who shot himself four years later (p. 84). Both deaths had an impact on the youngest brother, Gregory. As Bateson's biographer notes, "Gregory had grown up unnoticed. His had been a vicarious, hand-me-down sort of youth. In part he had felt John and Martin were more able. . . . Death now made Gregory sole heir to an ambiguous intellectual heritage in the natural sciences — personified by his father — and made him a central member of his family" (Lipset, 1980, p. 90).

Similarly, we saw the impact of the deaths of Virginia Woolf's parents (see p. 86) on her mental health. An event less likely to appear on a genogram (since family members are usually reluctant to reveal it) was the molestation of Virginia by her stepbrother. This traumatic violation had a profound effect on Virginia her whole life. (One of her books was entitled *A Room of One's Own*.)

The Kennedy family has had more than its share of losses, as can be seen in the genogram in Diagram 3.36. What is most striking about this family is the extraordinary number of premature deaths or tragedies. Four of the nine Kennedy children, as well as the spouse and the fiance of one of them, died before middle age; John had been previously given up for dead on at least three occasions; Rosemary had a lobotomy in her twenties; Kathleen and her fiancé were killed taking a dangerous plane ride just after a cut-off from her mother;

and Ted broke his back in a plane crash (seven months after John was shot) and was involved in an accident at Chappaquidick in which one person drowned (12 months after Robert was killed). Two grandchildren were responsible for car accidents in which someone was permanently paralyzed or seriously injured.

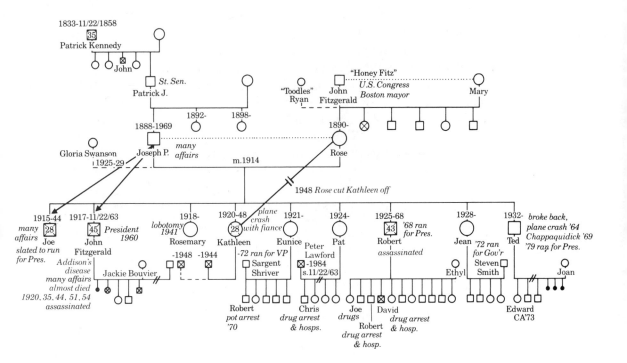

Diagram 3.36 Kennedy family — life changes, transitions and traumas

Often, critical life events in a family will send ripples throughout the family system, having an impact on the family in many different ways. This certainly seems to be the case in the Kennedy family following the assassinations of John and Robert. In addition to Ted's accidents mentioned above, Pat separated from her husband on the day of Jack's assassination. Of the 29 grandchildren, one has died of an overdose of drugs, one lost a leg through cancer, and at least four others have had drug arrests and/or psychiatric hospitalizations. This group includes four of the six oldest sons, suggesting perhaps the importance of sons and the pressures on the oldest in such a family. (See discussion on oldest sons under Category 1.)

There were at least two coincidences of the type mentioned above. Ted Kennedy had two life-threatening traumas (see above). Both events took place within the year following the death of his brothers John in 1963 and Robert in 1968. While such events could be totally unrelated, the studies of Holmes, Rahe, Masuda and their colleagues (Holmes & Rahe, 1967; Holmes & Masuda, 1974) indicate that stressful life events increase one's susceptibility to accidents.

The Roosevelt family (Diagram 3.37) is another example of a family which experienced a great deal of loss at a critical time in Eleanor's development. The time of Eleanor's birth was a hard one for her father's family. Elliot's mother had died a few months earlier. In addition, the first wife of Theodore Jr., Elliot's brother, had also died shortly before. Things did not improve in Eleanor's early years. Her father's drinking problem and hospitalization, as well as her parents' separation, were traumatic for her. Her brother died when she was five. Her mother died when she was eight and her father died when she was nine.

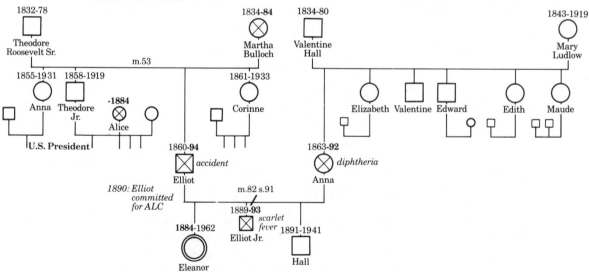

Diagram 3.37 Roosevelt family — loss and Eleanor's development

Seeing so many tragic events on the genogram leads one to speculate about the impact these events had on Eleanor's later development. Sometimes those born around the loss of grandparents may be more vulnerable to later dysfunction (Mueller & McGoldrick Orfanidis, 1976; Walsh, 1978), especially if they become the special focus of parental attention. Eleanor's experiences instead seemed to strengthen her character, while at the same time making her more sensitive to the tragedy of others. Eleanor reports having a rather awkward, isolated adolescence and a strong desire to have a family of her own to make up for the one she lost. This she was able to do when she met Franklin Roosevelt. Perhaps her early experience of loss and isolation propelled her to reach out to the world as she became an internationally known figure.

Tracking the impact of family events must occur within the context of normative expectations (Carter & McGoldrick, 1980). One must consider the ages and family structure at the time of the event. For instance, how children are affected by a critical event such as a loss of a parent depends on their level of emotional and cognitive development. An older child will have a different experience than a younger child. For example, Eleanor Roosevelt, as the oldest, took on a good deal of responsibility for her younger brother after her parents died.

As another example, Jefferson's deep attachment to his oldest daughter, Martha, who was ten at the time his beloved wife died, is not too surprising. She was old enough to be the most sensitive to his grief and was able to become something of a substitute for a time; she was also her mother's namesake.

Particularly traumatic for a family is the death of an infant or a young child. In preparing the genograms of famous people, we noticed that a quite a few were born shortly before or after the death of a sibling: Geraldine Ferraro (p. 92), F. Scott Fitzgerald (see p. 101), Sigmund Freud (p. 87), Henry Ford, Thomas Jefferson (p. 68), C. G. Jung (p. 60), Franz Kafka, Gustav Mahler, Eugene O'Neill (p. 81), and Harry Stack Sullivan (p. 117). One might attribute this solely to the higher child mortality rates of the past or speculate that the death of a child makes the surviving child even more "special" to the parents.

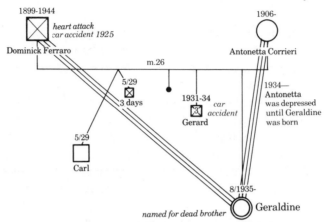

Diagram 3.38 Geraldine Ferraro—possible "replacement" child

A case in point is Geraldine Ferraro, the first woman vice presidential candidate for a major political party (Diagram 3.38). The miscarriage and the death of two of her siblings preceding her birth might make Geraldine's survival a special event for the family. In fact, she was named after her deceased brother, Gerald, who had lived for three years and was killed in a car accident in which the father was driving and the mother almost died as well. The mother was later told that having another baby was the best way to overcome her despondency. Usually a child born closest in time to the death or diagnosis of illness of the sibling is most vulnerable to becoming a replacement, especially if the child is of the same sex.

Finally, a "good" event can also have a powerful impact on a family. In fact, in many of the families we studied, the fame of one individual had profound repercussions for other members of the family. Not only was privacy often lost, but the children in the next generation also had a difficult legacy—a tough act to follow. Martin, the son of Sigmund Freud, said it well: "I have never had any ambition to rise to eminence. . . . I have been quite happy and content to bask in reflected glory. . . . The son of a genius remains the son of a genius, and his chances of winning human approval of anything he may do hardly exist if he attempts to make any claim to fame detached from that of his father" (Wallechinsky & Wallace, 1975, p. 948). This has not, however, stopped many from trying!

Anniversary Reactions

Certain so-called coincidences can be understood as anniversary reactions, i.e., family members react to the fact that the date is the anniversary of some critical or traumatic event. For example, a family member might become depressed at the same time each year around the date when a parent or sibling died, even though he or she often makes no conscious connection. This appears to have been the case in the suicide of Martin Bateson (see p. 84), who killed himself on his dead brother's birthday. Possibly this anniversary intensified his plight and feeling of loss to the point of suicide.

It is also interesting that both Thomas Jefferson and John Adams, the second and third presidents of the United States, died on the 50th anniversary of the signing of the Declaration of Independence, July 4, 1826. It was almost as if both of them waited until that anniversary to die. In fact, Adams' last words were, "Jefferson still survives," although he did not.

Sometimes, one event occurring on the anniversary of another event can intensify the meaning of both events. For example, John Kennedy died on the same day as his paternal great-grandfather (see p. 89). The great-grandfather's death was pivotal in that family since it left Kennedy's grandfather, P.J., at six months of age the only male in the family. Given that the earlier event left its mark on the family, the concurrence of John Kennedy's assassination might make November 22 a particularly emotionally potent day for the family.

One of the best documented examples of an anniversary reaction is that of George Engel (1975), a noted psychiatrist and internist who has written in detail about his own anniversary reactions following the fatal heart attack of his twin brother. The temporal connections become evident on the genogram shown in Diagram 3.39. Engel himself suffered a serious heart attack one year minus one day after the death of his brother, seemingly responding to the stress of the anniversary.

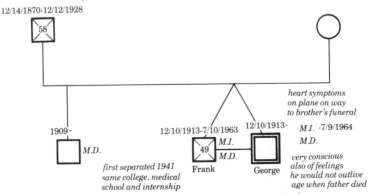

Diagram 3.39 George Engel – anniversary reaction

Engel reports experiencing another type of anniversary reaction, an anniversary of age rather than date. Engel's father died of a heart attack at the age of 58. As Engel himself approached this age he found himself becoming more anxious. He reports repeatedly mis-remembering the age of his father's death, fearing he would die at the same age. His experience led him to explore the psychological components of such family experiences and the mystifying way families often dissociate themselves from such emotional processes, e.g., forgetting the day or the year of significant events.

In other words, a type of anniversary reaction may be set up for corresponding events in the next generation of the family's life cycle. That is, as family members reach a certain point in the life cycle, they may expect the same thing to happen as happened at that point in the previous generation. For example, if a man's father cut off from his father when he left home, and then the man did the same with his father, he may expect his son to do the same when he reaches young adulthood. Another example would be a family in which the death of a key family member has followed shortly after each marriage for two generations. That particular life cycle transition will probably become a toxic point for the next generation, with members unconsciously fearing to repeat the events yet again.

Thus, it is important to scan the genogram not only for coincidences in time, but in date, age, and point in the family life cycle. Such coincidences point to the interconnectedness of events and the impact of change on family functioning. Once recognized, the family can be warned of the potency of particular anniversary reactions.

Social, Economic, and Political Events

Of course, family events do not occur in a vacuum. Family development must always be viewed against the background of its historical context, that is, the social, economic and political events that have influenced the well-being of the family. These include war, migration, economic depression, etc. It is important to connect the family events that appear on the genogram to the social, economic, and political context in which they occur (Elder, 1977; Runck, 1977). For example, a suicide in 1929 would probably have a different meaning than a suicide in another year, and a series of untimely deaths during World War II, such as occurred in the Kennedy family, would have a different meaning than the untimely deaths that occurred in that family at a later period.

The later tragic events in the Kennedy family, of course, took place against the backdrop of the historical and political era in which the family played such an important role. On a private level, the deaths of John and Robert were a tremendous loss for their families, but these tragic assassinations of two important leaders were also shared by the whole nation. It is likely that this merging of the private and personal experience of the family with the public historical experience has had a profound impact on the Kennedy's family adjustment to its loss, as shown by the next generation's evident difficulties.

Migration is another event that has great impact on a family. It is important to evaluate sibling relationships, for example, in the context of the timing of a family's migration. A family that migrates in the middle of the mother's child-bearing years may have two different sets of children, those born before and those born after the migration. The children born after the migration may have been raised in a much more hopeful context or, on the other hand, in a much more economically disadvantaged situation, as happened with many of the children from the first wave of the Cuban migration to the U.S. in the late fifties.

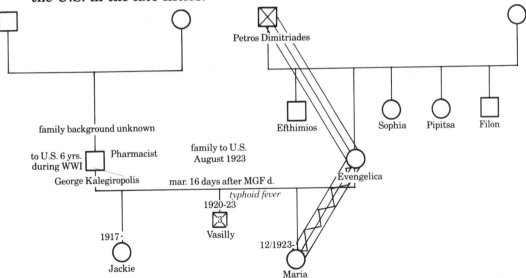

Diagram 3.40 Maria Callas—immigration child

Maria Callas (Diagram 3.40) is an example of a child who was the first child born after migration. The immigration appeared to have a major impact on the Callas family. Maria's parents had precipitously left Greece not long before her birth because an older brother had died of typhoid fever. In the new country they did not know the language and their adjustment was stressed further by the separation from their families and country. Under the circumstances Maria's father focused all his energy on making a living and her mother focused her energy on the most recently born child, Maria. It appears that Maria became a "special" child to her mother in part because her birth coincided with the stresses of the immigration experience, (in addition to her being born shortly after the family's only son died).

In the Blackwell family (see p. 67) only the youngest child, George Washington Blackwell, was born after the family's migration from England to the U.S. And, according to the information we have on the family, he was the only sibling not bound by the family's moralistic ideals and not involved in reform activities. Instead he became a pragmatic, financially successful businessman, who ended up handling the investments of the rest of the family (Horn, 1980, pp. 138–9).

In sum, tracking critical events and changes in family functioning allows us to make systemic connections between seeming coincidences, assess the impact of traumatic changes on family functioning and its vulnerability to future stresses, track anniversary reactions, and then try to understand such events in the larger social, economic and political context.

CATEGORY 5: RELATIONAL PATTERNS AND TRIANGLES

Relational patterns in families have been variously characterized as "close," "fused," "hostile," "conflictual," "distant," "cut-off," etc. The complexity of family relationships is infinite. In addition, of course, relationships change over time. In spite of such complexity, the genogram can often suggest relational patterns to be further explored.

Obviously, the smallest human system is a two-person system. Genograms can be analyzed in terms of dyadic relationships, with

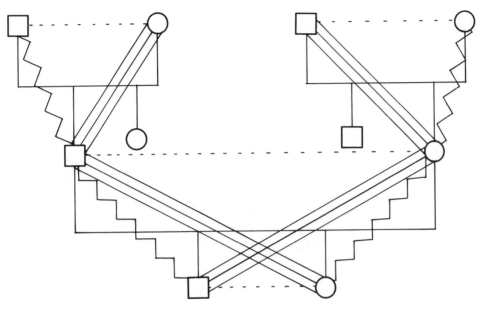

Diagram 3.41 Multigenerational dyadic relationships

relationship lines depicting these patterns in at least a crude way. One can then look for repeated dyadic patterns throughout the system, as in Diagram 3.41.

If one focuses simply on the relationships in this genogram, one notices that in each generation all sons have a conflictual relationships with their fathers and close relationships with their mothers, while daughters have the opposite – conflictual relationships with their mothers and close relationships with their fathers. Meanwhile, all the couples have distant or conflictual relationships. In other words, there is a complementary pattern of marital distance and of same-sex conflicts and cross-sex alliances between the generations. One might then predict that the son and daughter in the third generation would repeat this pattern of distant marriages, conflict with same-sexed children, and closeness with the opposite-sexed children.

However, another level of analysis would link these dyadic relationships and see each as a function of the others. That is, we can look at the family system as a set of interlocking triangles. From this perspective father's distance from mother is a function of his closeness with his daughter and of mother's conflict with the daughter. One could hypothesize the same for any threesome in this system: that the functioning of any two is bound up with the interrelationships of the three in a predictable way. One of these triangles

is highlighted in the genogram. This brings us to the subject of triangles (Bowen, 1978; Caplow, 1968; Fogarty, 1973; Friedman, 1985).

Triangles

While it would be impossible in this short handbook to explain
all the complexities of systemic thinking which underlie the interpretation of relational patterns on genograms, there are a number
of common relational configurations which we offer as schema for
interpreting genograms.

Our primary focus is on triangles, or sets of three relationships
in which the functioning of each dyad is dependent on and influences
the other two. The formation of triangles in families involves two
people bringing (triangling) a third into their relationship. This usually serves the function of lessening difficulties in the initial dyad. For
example, two family members may join in "helping" a third, who is
labeled "victim," or gang up against a third, who is in this case labeled "villain." It is the collusion of the two in relation to the third
that is the defining characteristic of a triangle (Bowen, 1978). The
behavior of any one member of a triangle is thus a function of the
behavior of the other two.

Any triangle tends to be part of a larger systemic pattern of interlocking triangles as well. Thus, a child's tantrum with an over-
burdened mother is not only a function of the relationship between
mother and child, but may also be a function of the relationship between mother and distant father, or between those two and an over-
involved paternal grandfather, or between one or several adults and
a precocious older sibling, to mention just a few of the possibilities.

In Bowen's conceptual framework, healthy development involves
differentiating to the point where one can function independently
in each relationship and not automatically fall into a certain pattern
of relating to one person because of that person's relationship with
another person. When there is high tension in a system, it is common for two people to join in relating to a third to relieve stress.
Differentiation means reaching the point where one relates on an
individualized basis rather than on the basis of the relationship that
person has to someone else. Thus, a daughter would be able to have
a close relationship with her mother even if her father, with whom
she was also close, was in conflict with her mother.

The genogram is a valuable interpretive tool for inferring possible triangles based on partial knowledge of family relationships.

Parent/child Triangles

When tension develops between two parents, they may resolve it by joining together to focus on their child. Regardless of the specific emotional pattern displayed (anger, love, clinging dependency), it is the joining together of the two people in relation to a third that defines triangular relationships. Genograms are an extremely handy tool for recognizing such triangles because structural patterns, life-cycle information, and specific data on dyadic relationships often make obvious the predictable threesomes who are likely to become triangulated.

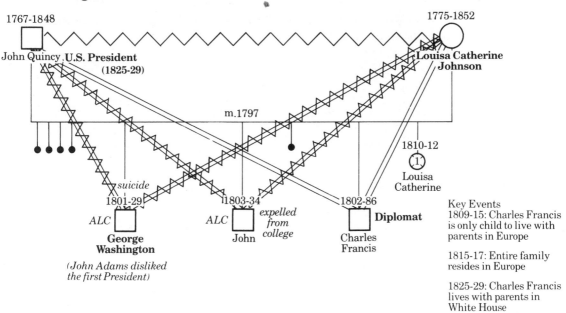

1767-1848
John Quincy, **U.S. President**
(1825-29)

1775-1852
Louisa Catherine Johnson

m.1797

1810-12
①
Louisa
Catherine

suicide
1801-29
ALC George Washington
(John Adams disliked the first President)

1803-34
ALC John
expelled from college

1802-86
Charles Francis
Diplomat

Key Events
1809-15: Charles Francis is only child to live with parents in Europe

1815-17: Entire family resides in Europe

1825-29: Charles Francis lives with parents in White House

Diagram 3.42 John Quincy Adams – triangles

For example, we know that John Quincy Adams and his wife, Louisa Catherine, were intensively focused on their sons, worrying about them constantly, as indicated by the lines of fusion on the genogram shown in Diagram 3.42. Seeing this on a genogram should suggest possible marital tension, which has been refocused on the children. As their biographer points out, "Louisa later wondered if she had been more mature, she might have seen that her husband's 'unnecessary harshness and severity of character' would make life with him a perpetual trial to her own joyous and affection-craving spirit" (Nagel, 1983, p. 65). And "Louisa's trials were once caught in a cry she uttered to her husband: 'I can neither live with or without you.' One of her greatest stresses arose from the different views she and John Quincy had about raising children" (p. 101). It is not surprising, given an understanding of triangles, that as the sons grew older, the two oldest children did poorly and became a negative focus for the parents (George eventually committed suicide and John was expelled from college), while Charles Francis became a positive focus (as a successful statesman). This is not unusual in such child-focused families, where "good" and "bad" children are often juxtaposed (see Category 6, Family Balance and Imbalance, for further discussion). Interestingly enough, John Quincy saw fit to name his oldest son after a man his father reportedly loathed. Given this and the usual pressures on the oldest sons in this family, it makes some sense that George Washington Adams became part of a negative triangle with his parents which eventually ended in suicide.

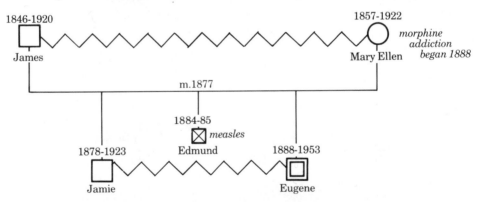

Diagram 3.43 Eugene O'Neill – sibling rivalry

Sometimes intense sibling rivalry will appear, as shown on the genogram of Eugene O'Neill (Diagram 3.43). The brothers maintained an intense competitive relationship throughout their lives (Jamie died at age 45). Seeing this on the genogram should suggest possible marital tension, the conflict in one generation both deflecting and reflecting conflict in the previous generation. In fact, we know that the parents had a difficult and stormy relationship throughout their lives. Perhaps the tension between the brothers was exacerbated by the fact that Jamie was blamed for Edmund's death (he had exposed him to measles) and Eugene was blamed for his mother's addiction (she started taking morphine during his birth). One might hypothesize here that the sibling conflict reflects the parental conflict and, in addition, helps the parents distract themselves from their own difficulties.

A very common triangular pattern occurs when one parent draws the child into a collusion against the other parent, who becomes an outsider. This usually appears on the genogram as a child's having an intensely fused relationship with one parent, an intensely conflictual relationship with the other parent, or both.

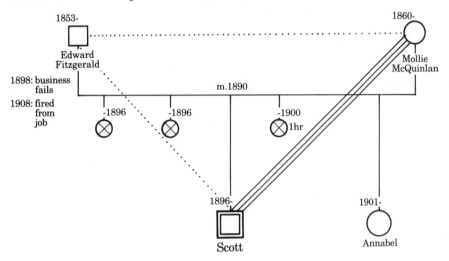

Diagram 3.44 F. Scott Fitzgerald – fused relationship with his mother

A good example of this is the intense relationship of F. Scott Fitzgerald and his mother (Diagram 3.44). As one biographer describes it, "She spoiled Scott in every way possible, catering to his smallest whim. . . . As Scott grew older, his mother became increasingly overprotective and eccentric" (Stavola, 1979, p. 25). Seeing this on the genogram should raise the question of the role of the father. Scott's birth was particularly important to his mother since it shortly followed the loss of two daughters to epidemics. We know that the father's business failed in 1898; then he lost the last of a series of jobs in 1908, and remained unemployed, living off his wife's family. Perhaps Mollie, disappointed with her husband, focused on her son. The father probably disengaged from the family. The son, on his part, had ambivalent feelings about his father. He loved him but did not respect or pay much attention to him. One might hypothesize here the triangle of an intense mother and son relationship and an under-involved husband/father. The mother's focus on the son may have served to distract her from the loss of her daughters and her disappointment with her husband.

Incidentally, such a close relationship with one's mother does not seem to be a necessarily damaging experience (McCullogh, 1983). We found it to be common to many of the famous people we investigated, including Sigmund Freud, Franklin Roosevelt, Harry Truman, Frank Lloyd Wright, Douglas McArthur, and Jimmy Carter, to mention just a few. In most of these cases, the father was either a weak figure, a failure, or absent during most of the child's growing-up years.

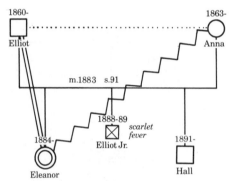

Diagram 3.45 Eleanor Roosevelt—triangle

The genogram of Eleanor Roosevelt (Diagram 3.45) presents an example of another type of parent/child triangle. Eleanor remembered having a special relationship with her father in her early years and often not getting along with her mother. One might hypothesize here a triangle in which Eleanor took her father's side against her mother. We do know that Eleanor's mother was disturbed and upset by her husband's drinking and there was at one point a marital separation. The child in this situation may even be used by one parent to express or act out feelings to the other, and Eleanor may have been used in this way by her father.

Finally, a child may be caught in a loyalty conflict. In this type of relational pattern the parents are in severe conflict. The child may attempt to placate or mediate between the parents, a precarious position indeed. Since this type of parent/child triangle is so common in cases of divorce and remarriage, it will be discussed in that section.

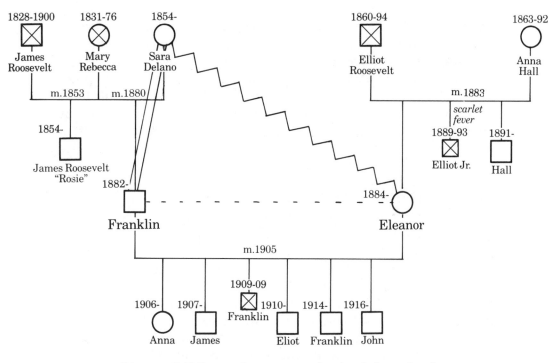

Diagram 3.46 Roosevelt genogram showing in-law triangle

Common Couple Triangles

In addition to children, a couple may include other persons or things as part of their triangle. The most common couple triangle is perhaps the in-law triangle. Classically, this involves a favorite son, his mother, and his wife, as seen in the marriage of Franklin and Eleanor Roosevelt (Diagram 3.46). Franklin's mother, Sara Delano, was highly invested in her only son, particularly following the early death of her husband. This is indicated by the lines of fusion on the genogram. One might thus predict an in-law triangle when Franklin married. In fact, Sara objected strongly to Franklin's courting and eventually marrying Eleanor. She competed with Eleanor even before the marriage, working to get Franklin to visit her rather than Eleanor. After the marriage, there was periodic conflict between Eleanor and her mother-in-law, Franklin and his mother, and Eleanor and Franklin.

The in-law triangle may play itself out in a variety of ways. The spouses may divert their own conflicts by focusing on what is wrong with the husband's mother. Or the wife may blame the mother-in-law for her husband's inadequacies, while the mother-in-law blames the daughter-in-law for keeping her "darling boy" away. And the husband may enjoy letting his mother and his wife go at it; he probably has difficulty dealing with both of them. It is a case of "Let's you and her fight." Of course, in-law triangles can naturally occur between two spouses and any of their four parents, but the wife often takes a more central and involved role and thus becomes the focus of stress in this situation.

Another common couple triangle involves an affair. Clearly, an extramarital relationship has implications for a marriage and can become a major area of concern even if the marriage survives. The affair may relieve some of the tension of a conflictual relationship by giving one of the partners an outlet or it may divert the couple from underlying problems. The triangulated affair may be ongoing or in the past, as with Eugene O'Neill's parents. As seen on the genogram (Diagram 3.28, p. 81), James O'Neill had two affairs preceding his marriage to Mary Ellen. The first woman committed suicide when James broke off the relationship. The second relationship resulted in a paternity suit a number of years later when Nettie Walsh claimed that James was the father of her son. The scandal surrounding the paternity suit remained an issue throughout James and Mary Ellen's marriage.

Wilhelm Reich's genogram shows how triangles can reflect tragic patterns when an affair is going on in a family. Wilhelm discovered his mother having an affair with his tutor and told his father who then confronted the wife. She committed suicide in response. One might think of Reich's later espousal of sexuality in all forms as an attempt to make up for the disastrous results of his own part in that family's triangle (Diagram 3.47).

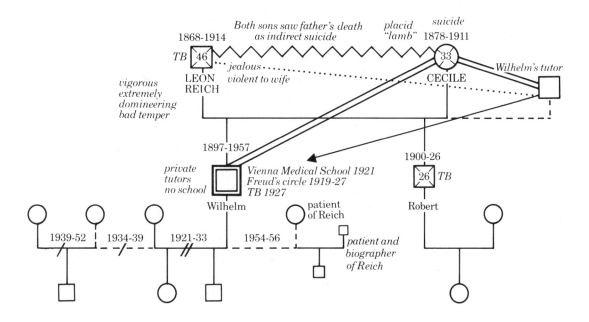

Diagram 3.47 Reich family

The investment of a spouse outside the marriage may be in an affair, work, hobbies, the bottle, etc., but the impact is the same. For example, the closer the husband gets to the affair, the job, or the booze, the more negative the wife becomes towards both him and the object of his "affections"; the more negative the wife becomes, the closer the husband moves to the girlfriend, the job, or the booze. It is important to note that triangling occurs with objects as well as people. When this happens, it should be noted on the genogram. One common object of triangulation in the modern American family is television, with one family member often becoming more involved with the TV as the other tries to pull him or her away.

Triangles in Divorced and Remarried Families

When separation or divorce appears on a genogram, the possibility of certain predictable relational patterns should be explored. For ex-

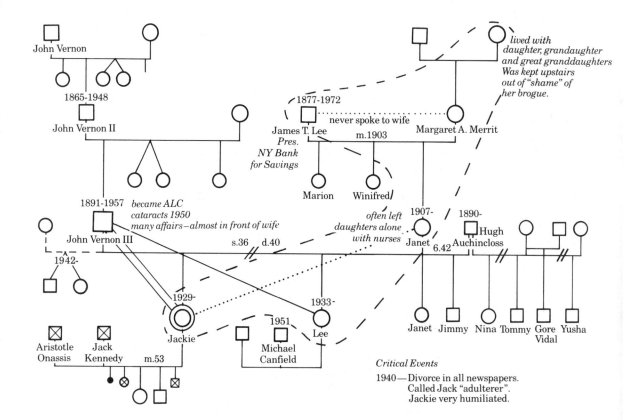

Diagram 3.48 Bouvier – family triangling after divorce

ample, children often idealize the missing parent, blaming the present parent for the loss of the other. This seemed to be the case of Jackie Bouvier Kennedy (Diagram 3.48). Her parents had finally separated in 1936 when her mother could no longer tolerate her husband's philandering and drinking. Jackie remained lovingly attached to her father in spite of repeated disappointments in the relationship with him.

When one or both parents remarry, there are additional predictable triangles to explore. Perhaps one of the reasons such triangles are so easy to identify on the genograms of remarried families is that the structure of the family (as mentioned in Category 1), rather than the personalities of the participants, usually defines the situation.

In other words, the triangles are somewhat normative. Children are basically never prepared to lose a parent, however the original family ends, whether by death or divorce. Parents are not replaceable. The other parent is always in the picture. Thus the insider-outsider structural pattern in remarried families is endemic to the situation and tends to create triangles.

The following schematic genograms demonstrate some of the predictable triangles in remarried families. One possibility is that the children in a family with a natural father and a stepmother do not get along with the stepmother. This is not surprising. The stepmother can never replace the natural mother and the child's alliance will usually be with the biological parent rather than the stepparent. For the father in this situation the new wife offers new hope after his loss. For the child she is a threat: She may take the parent away.

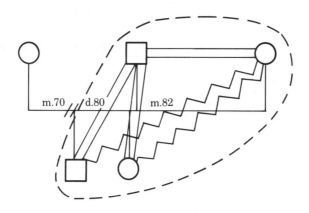

Diagram 3.49 Children, natural father and stepmother

Two different types of triangles are likely in this situation. One is a triangle involving the children, the natural father, and the stepmother (Diagram 3.49). There is hostility between the children and the new wife (the "wicked" stepmother). The stepmother often feels that her spouse gives more attention to his children than he does to her, and the husband is usually caught in a loyalty conflict be-

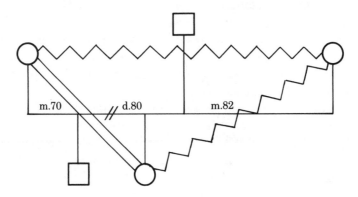

Diagram 3.50 Children, stepmother and natural mother

tween his wife and his children. The second triangle involves the children, the stepmother, and the natural mother (Diagram 3.50). The children may resent the stepmother's efforts to replace their natural mother. The new wife feels unaccepted in her own home and the natural mother may feel threatened by the new wife. It is not uncommon for overt conflict to occur between the mother and stepmother in this triangle.

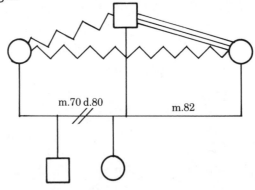

Diagram 3.51 Husband, new wife and excluded ex-wife

Another variation on this theme is the common triangle involving the ex-spouses and the husband's new wife. There is tension between the couple and the ex-wife, with the ex-wife on the outside. Two types of triangles are likely here. The new couple may band together against the ex-spouse, seeing her as the cause of all their problems (Diagram 3.51). Or the new and old wife may have overt con-

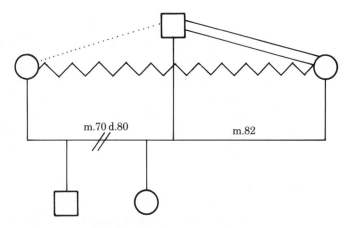

Diagram 3.52 Husband and conflicting new and ex-wives

flicts, with the husband perhaps even encouraging his new wife to fight the old battles for him (Diagram 3.52). Of course, triangles also occur with a natural mother, her children, and a stepfather. However, because our culture places greater expectations on motherhood than on fatherhood, stepmothers generally seem to have a more difficult experience (McGoldrick & Carter, 1980).

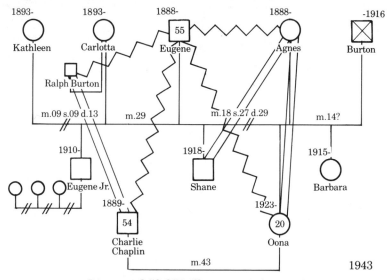

Diagram 3.53 O'Neill—remarried triangle

Another relational pattern in a remarried family is seen on the genogram of Eugene O'Neill, who had a poor relationship with his children by his second wife (Diagram 3.53). O'Neill separated from

Agnes when their youngest child, Oona, was only three and had little
to do with her or Shane after that. This may have been partly due
to continual resentment towards their mother for what he felt were
exorbitant alimony payments. When Oona married Charlie Chaplin,
O'Neill refused to have anything to do with her ever again. One biography (Gelb & Gelb, 1970) suggests that this had something to do
with Chaplin's being a very good friend of the ex-husband of O'Neill's
wife, Carlotta. The triangles multiply quickly in remarried families.

Finally, the in-laws are not always neutral on the subject of remarriage. For example, there may be a great deal of tension between
the husband's mother and his new wife. Thus, the grandparent generation often gets involved in remarried triangles, intensifying the
process by joining with their adult child, especially against the ex-
spouse, whom they may blame for the divorce.

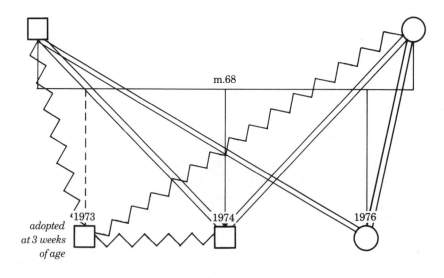

Diagram 3.54 Nuclear family triangle involving foster/adopted children

Triangles in Families with Foster or Adopted Children

Many parent/child triangles are particularly common when one or more of the children is a foster or adopted child. When there are also biological children in the family, the adopted child may have a unique position in the family. In the family shown in Diagram 3.54, for example, tension between the parents—perhaps because of their failure to have their own children, perhaps for other reasons—was present before the child was adopted. This led the couple to focus intensely and negatively on the adopted child, who was treated as an outsider, serving to distract the family from other concerns.

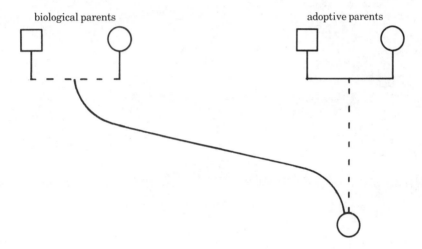

biological parents   adoptive parents

Diagram 3.55 Triangle of adoptee with adoptive and biological parents

In many ways, families with foster or adopted children are like remarried families in that there are two families involved: the caretaking family and the biological family. This is true whether the biological parents are known or not, since people can triangulate a memory or idea as well as actual people. For example, consider the genogram shown in Diagram 3.55. Several triangles are possible here. The child may play one set of parents against the other. The caretaking parents may blame the biological parents for their difficulties (bad genes). Or, if there are also biological children, rivalry for the parents' attention and competition between the adopted and biological children may occur.

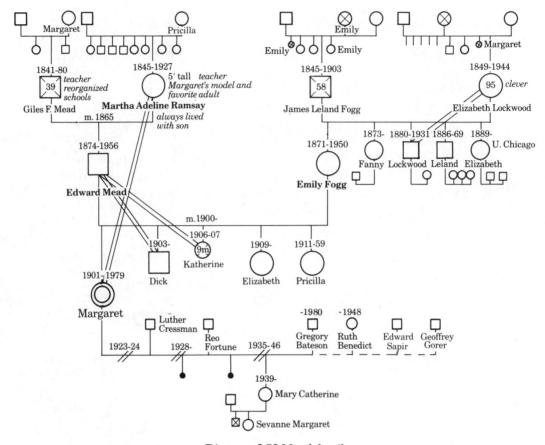

Diagram 3.56 Mead family

Multigenerational Triangles

As mentioned earlier, triangles can cross many generations. Probably the most common three-generational triangle is one in which a grandparent and grandchild ally against the parents. In both the Mead family genogram (Diagram 3.56) and the King family genogram (Diagram 3.20, p. 64), we see that Margaret and Martin had very close relationships with their grandparents. Seeing this on a genogram suggests the hypothesis of a triangle where a parent may be an ineffectual outsider to a cross-generational alliance. Such multigenerational triangles are likely to develop if one parent dies or leaves because of separation or divorce. One of the most common patterns occurs when a single mother and her children share a household with her parents. The mother may lose power as the grandparents take over child-rearing responsibilities or as a grandparent-grandchild alliance forms against her.

Of course, the pattern of triangles across generations can become quite complex. For example, let's look again at the genogram on p. 97. This was taken from a schema for understanding schizophrenics and their families that McGoldrick worked out with a colleague some years ago (Mueller & McGoldrick Orfanidis, 1976). The hypothesized pattern illustrates the potential for children to fall into triangular patterns set in motion long before their birth. In this example the index person or schizophrenic is involved in a fixed triangular relationship involving emotional fusion with the opposite-sexed parent and a negative or minimal relationship with the same-sexed parent. The IP becomes the caretaker for the opposite-sexed parent by letting this parent take care of him/her. This pattern is a mirror image of the triangles between the parental and grandparental generation, since the schizophrenic's mother was the emotional caretaker for her father and had a poor relationship with her mother, while the schizophrenic's father was the emotional caretaker of his mother and had a poor relationship with his father. Throughout the system spouse relationships tend to be less intense than parent/child relationships, and same-sexed relationships tend to be poor while opposite-sexed relationships are emotionally fused.

Relationships Outside the Family

There tends to be a correlation between the intensity of relational patterns within a family and a family's relationships with outsiders, i.e., the greater the intensity of relationships within a family, the more closed that system may become to relations outside the family. Thus, if one sees on the genogram patterns of fused relationships or intense triangles, one might then investigate the family's boundary with the outside world.

For example, in the Bronte family (see p. 73), only Charlotte had any ongoing relationships outside the immediate family. The other three siblings who lived to adulthood all died within a nine-month period, one after another, almost as though their fusion made it impossible for them to live without each other. The genogram offers a number of clues about the boundaries of this family. None of the siblings except Charlotte ever left home for more than a brief period.

In fact, the Brontes usually became ill whenever they were away from home. The two sisters who died in childhood developed their fatal illnesses during their first period away from home and died within a short period of each other.

In sum, the genogram allows the clinician to detect intense relationships in a family and, given the family's structure and position in the life cycle, to hypothesize about the important triangular patterns and boundaries of that family. Understanding such triangular patterns is essential in planning clinical intervention. "Detriangling" is an important clinical process through which family members are coached to free themselves from rigid triangular patterns.

CATEGORY 6: FAMILY BALANCE AND IMBALANCE

The last category involves an analysis of genogram data on a higher level of abstraction and thus encompasses the earlier principles. In other words, one can potentially see balance and imbalance in all the patterns mentioned earlier, particularly in family structure, roles, level of functioning, and resources.

Balance and imbalance speak to the functional whole of a family system. Family systems are not homogenous and contrasting characteristics are usually present in the same family. In well-functioning families, such characteristics usually balance out one another. For example, we have already discussed the complementary fit of oldest and youngest, where the oldest's tendency to be caretaker balances the youngest's tendency to be taken care of by others (see Category 1, Family Structure).

Patterns of balance and imbalance can best be seen by looking for contrasts and characteristics that "stick out." The clinician then asks: How do these contrasts and idiosyncrasies fit into the total functional whole? What balances have been obtained and what stresses are present in the system due to a lack of balance? For example, if one person is doing poorly in a family in which everyone else is doing well, the imbalance immediately brings up the question of the role the dysfunction plays in the total system. There are several areas where balance or imbalance are most likely to occur, which are discussed below.

The Family Structure

Family structure can suggest possible patterns of balance and imbalance. There is, as we discussed earlier, a degree of marital complementarity related to sibling position; that is, all things being equal, a youngest with opposite-sexed siblings will do better with an oldest with opposite-sexed siblings than either will do with a spouse who has the same sibling position or with only same-sexed siblings. Theoretically, partners from opposite sibling positions complement each other. An oldest is used to younger siblings and being in charge, while a youngest is used to being dominated and taken care of by older siblings.

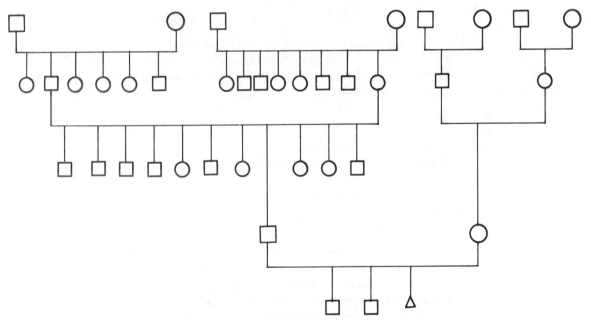

Diagram 3.57 Spouses from small and large families

Sometimes, differences in family structure may be seen over a number of generations. For example, in Diagram 3.57, there is a multigenerational contrast in the family structure for the two spouses.

This genogram is graphically lopsided. One spouse comes from a large family, while the other spouse was an only child of two only children. Such a contrast in structure could lead to both balance and imbalance. On the one hand, each spouse may be attracted to the experience of the other: one to the privacy of a small family and the other to the diversity of a large family. However, the imbalance between the large number of relatives on one side and the paucity of relatives on the other may create problems for the marital partners. One may be used to playing to a crowd and engaging in multiple relationships, while the other needs a more exclusive, private relationship with the spouse.

Another structural issue involving balance occurs when one spouse comes from a family where divorce and remarriage are common and the other comes from a long line of intact households. Seeing this structural contrast on the genogram might cue the clinician to explore the spouses' different expectations about marriage.

Roles

In well-functioning families, members take a variety of different roles: caretaker, dependent, provider, spokesman, etc. Sometimes from the genogram it will be evident that there are too many actors for one particular role. For example, Harry Stack Sullivan (Diagram 3.58) grew up as an only child in a household with many parental figures. In addition to Harry, there were his mother, his father, his mother's mother, and, at times, his mother's sister in the household. It is clear that there were many adults vying for the role of caretaker of the only child.

Similarly, a single family leader may have responsibility for an inordinate number of family members, as Ted Kennedy does since his brothers' deaths (see p. 89). Since Ted is the sole surviving male member of his generation in the family, he has had a special role in the three other fatherless households, as well as responsibility for his own family. A clinician seeing this family would need to explore how a balance has been worked out and what other resources have been brought in to help in taking care of the many children involved.

In modern marriages, role allocation is seldom based solely on gender and is often shared. Thus, both parents may be caretakers, providers, and spokespeople for the family. However, this balance

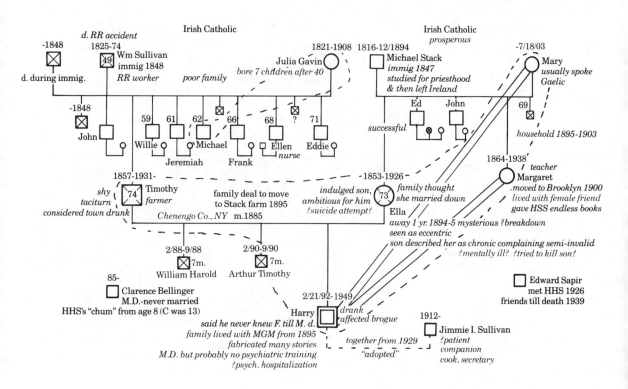

Diagram 3.58 Harry Stack Sullivan family—many figures for one role

is not achieved automatically or easily, and so this may be an area of conflict particularly in dual-career families.

Level and Style of Functioning

Family members operate with different styles and at different levels of functioning. Often these patterns are balanced so that the functions of different family members all fit in a particular adaptive form. Again, we scan the genogram for contrasts and idiosyncrasies in functioning which may help to explain how the system functions as a whole.

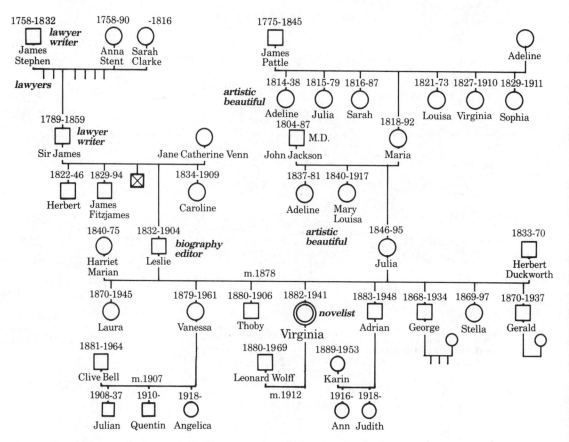

Diagram 3.59 Virginia Woolf—inheritor of two complementary family styles

In any new family, different styles and ways of relating to the world need to fit together. The result may be more or less complementary and growth-enhancing for the offspring. For example, Virginia Woolf (Diagram 3.59) felt she was the fortunate inheritor of two different, but complementary, styles from her mother's and father's sides. On her father's side, family members seemed to be bold, pragmatic, legalistic, and writers of persuasive political arguments. On her mother's side, family members tended to be beautiful, artistic, stylish, and somewhat unapproachable. Virginia felt she was able to combine and balance these two styles in her own life and work.

Certain balances in families may also lead to or allow dysfunction in a family system. For example, we often see on a genogram a complementary pattern of alcoholics married to spouses who are over-

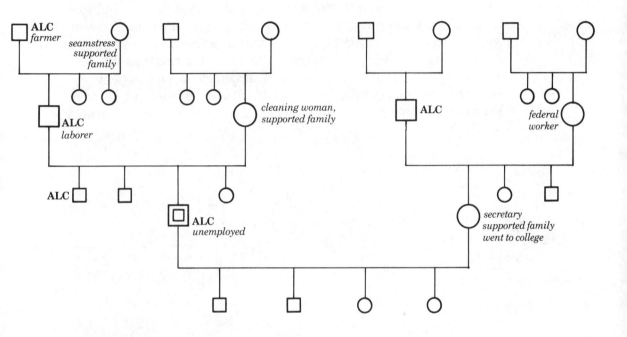

Diagram 3.60 Alcohol Problems: Over and under functioning

functioners (Bepko & Krestan, 1985), as in Diagram 3.60. Here, an overresponsible spouse may balance an underresponsible spouse, as is the rule in marriages with an alcoholic partner. Since alcoholic behavior by its nature leads to underresponsibility, the other partner necessarily becomes overresponsible; otherwise the couple would split apart. Many times the mutual need of the overresponsible partner to be a caretaker and of the other to be taken care of stabilizes the relationship. At times the whole family may become organized in this complementary way around the dysfunction of one member.

An example of a seeming imbalance of functioning is the Adams family. As mentioned earlier (see p. 78), the Adams history is one of great successes coupled with dismal failures in each generation. For example, John Adams was a president while his brother was a poor, ineffectual farmer. His son, John Quincy Adams, also became president, while one sister had a disastrous marriage, the other was an unhappy spinster, and the two younger brothers were quite un-

successful, both having unhappy marriages and serious problems
with alcohol. In the next generation, the oldest son committed suicide, the next son was expelled from college, and the youngest son
was a successful diplomat. In the fourth generation, the oldest
daughter had an unhappy marriage, the oldest son was unambitious,
and the youngest son was an unhappy, eccentric misanthrope. However, this last son, Brooks, as well as his two older brothers, Charles
Francis and Henry, were all famous and accomplished writers and
family historians.

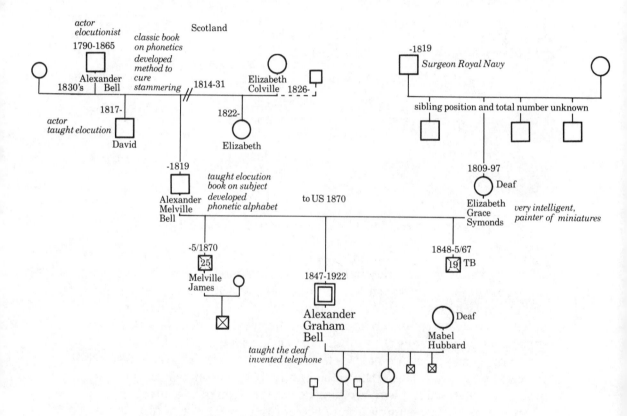

Diagram 3.61 Alexander Graham Bell family – function of deafness in family

Sometimes when there is a good deal of dysfunction in one area,
the family will find ways to compensate for common difficulties. This
seems to have been the case with the family of Alexander Graham
Bell, the inventor of the telephone (Diagram 3.61). The difficulty in

this family was deafness. Both Bell's mother and wife were almost totally deaf. Three generations of males in the family: Bell himself, his father and uncle, and his grandfather all specialized in speech projection and elocution. Bell's grandfather wrote a classic text on phonetic speech, and both Bell's father and uncle devoted themselves to teaching their father's methods. The family was a highly inventive one. When Alexander was a young teenager, his father suggested that he and his brother develop a talking machine. They studied the mechanisms of speech so well that the instrument they developed annoyed a neighbor, who thought he heard a baby crying. Some members specialized in speech and hearing, compensating for those who could not speak or hear at all.

In analyzing possible patterns of functioning in families, it is essential to determine whether there is a fit or a balance in the system. Do extreme contrasts between family members maintain the stability of the system or are they pushing the family toward a different equilibrium? At times a system breaks down not because of the dysfunction of one or two members but because of the burnout of caretakers who previously created a balanced fit in the system. In the case of chronic illness, family members are frequently able to mobilize themselves in the short term for support of the dysfunctional person, but are not able to maintain such behavior over the long term.

Resources

Finally, family members often differ in resources such as money, health and vigor, skills, meaningful work, and support systems. When extreme differences in these areas appear on the genogram, it important to explore how the system handles the imbalance.

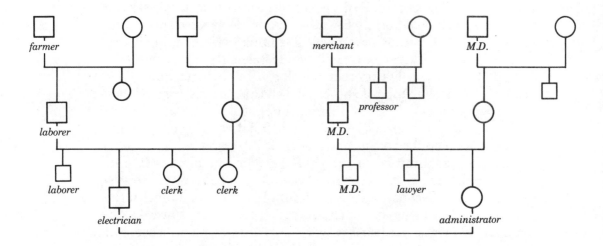

Diagram 3.62 Couple with different occupational backgrounds

In the genogram shown in Diagram 3.62, the spouses differ in class and occupational background. Immediately questions arise: How do the spouses handle their differences in class and background? How do they handle their different levels of income and expectations about standards of living? Is there an important balance or imbalance in some other area? Is there a difference in values? Of course, other family members come into play as well. How did the two different families feel about the marriage? Was there approval or disapproval for the match? The genogram should alert the clinician to these possible issues.

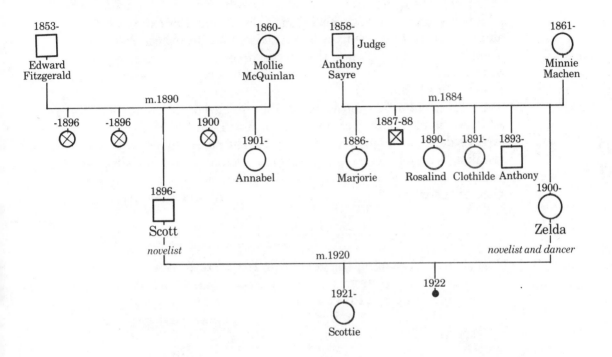

Diagram 3.63 Scott and Zelda Fitzgerald

Sometimes, contrasts in career success can lead to problems, as it did in the Fitzgerald family (Diagram 3.63). When Scott first began to write novels, Zelda was quite willing to sacrifice her personal ambition and play the role of supporting wife. However, she eventually became dissatisfied with living only in his reflected glory and expressed her desires to both write and pursue a career in dance. At first, Scott encouraged her in this. But when she began to be published, he felt she had stolen his material and jealously forbade her to pursue her writing career. It would appear that Zelda's efforts at self-expression had shifted the balance between them. Great success for one spouse should always raise questions about the other spouse's adaptation or contribution to this.

Differences in resources can also become problematic when one sibling becomes more successful than the others. For example, if one sibling in a family becomes a physician and all others do poorly, there is often an imbalance; the successful one cannot meet the needs of the siblings and they in turn resent both her or his success and the lack of support. When resources (emotional as well as financial) are lacking, one frequently sees siblings cutting off, particularly around the caretaking of a parent or an ill sibling. There may be endless debates about who did more for the person in need. In other families, where most siblings are doing well and only one sibling or one parent is in need, it may be easier to develop a satisfactory balance of resources without unduly taxing any one member.

In sum, reading the genogram for patterns of contrast and balance in family structure, roles, functioning, and resources allows the clinician to derive hypotheses about how the family is adapting to imbalances that may be stressing the system.

4

CLINICAL USES
OF THE GENOGRAM

We have only begun to tap the rich clinical potential of the genogram. Here we will focus on its use in family therapy and family practice.

THE GENOGRAM IN FAMILY THERAPY

The genogram arose out of the practice of family therapy; therefore, not surprisingly, most of its applications have been pioneered in this field. Genograms have been used in many different ways by different therapists. We will focus on four specific uses: 1) to engage the whole family; 2) to unblock the system; 3) to clarify family patterns; and 4) to reframe and detoxify family issues. A comprehensive discussion of the clinical application of genograms is beyond the scope of this book, and the following should be seen only as suggestive.

Engaging the Family

In order to be of help, the family therapist must first engage the family in the therapeutic process. Preferably, as many relevant family members as possible will be involved so that the clinician will better see the problem in its familial context. The genogram interview usually provides a practical way of engaging the whole family in a systemic approach to treatment.

Genogram interviewing shows interest in the whole family system. The process of mapping family information on the genogram implies that a larger picture of the situation is needed to understand the problem and conveys a major systemic assumption: All family members are involved in whatever happens to any member. It also suggests the ongoing connectedness of the family, both with the past and with the future.

Equally important, the genogram interview often allows the therapist to build rapport with family members around issues of specific concern to the family. Genogram questioning goes to the heart of family experiences: birth, illness, death, and intense relationships. Its structure provides an orienting framework for discussion of the full range of family experiences and for tracking and bringing into focus difficult issues such as family illnesses, losses, and conflicts.

Genograms often provide almost instant access to complex, emotionally loaded family material. However, the structure of the genogram interview seems to elicit such information in a relatively non-threatening way. Neutral, matter-of-fact gathering of information to complete a family diagram often leads to matter-of-fact giving of information. Even the most guarded person, quite unresponsive to open-ended questions, may be willing to discuss his or her family in such a structured format (McGoldrick, 1977; Wachtel, 1982).

There is something impressive about not just gathering information but also displaying it to the family in an organized, graphic way. Some clinicians will display the genogram to the family either on the blackboard (Carter, 1982) or on large note pads (Bradt, 1980). Genograms seem to possess a certain mystique and thus may be an important "hook" for some families. Wachtel (1982) has argued that their power may be something like psychological tests, which add weight and credibility to inferences a clinician may make about family patterns.

Sometimes, while a genogram is taken, one spouse may appear bored or the children become restless (Wachtel, 1982). The key to gaining receptivity with such families is to build connections carefully outward from the presenting problem in a way that demonstrates the relevance of the larger family context to the family's immediate concerns. In our experience there have been occasional, but infrequent, situations in which family members have been so resistant to discussions of genogram information that we have had to leave the subject until we found another way of engaging them. In those situations when we have eventually succeeded in building a relationship with the family, we have found that the resistance came from painful memories of family experiences, for example, the stigma of a parent who committed suicide or was in a mental hospital.

Unblocking the System

When a family comes in with a problem, it has often adopted its own view of the problem and what needs to be changed. This is often a rigid, nonsystemic view based on the belief that only one person, the symptomatic one, needs to change. Any effort to move directly into other problematic areas of the family will often be blocked by vehement denial of other family difficulties.

The genogram can be useful in working with such rigid systems. The genogram interview organizes questioning around key family life experiences: birth, marriage, life transitions, illness and death. Collecting information on these events can open up a rigid family system and help clients get in touch with paralyzing blocked emotional and interpersonal issues. Sometimes, seemingly innocuous questions may provoke an intense reaction, as when a client burst into tears after being asked how many siblings he had. The question had stirred up memories of his favorite brother, who had died in a drowning accident. Ostensibly simple questions may also unearth family secrets, such as when the question, "How long have you been married?" leads to embarrassment or concealment for a couple who conceived their first child before marriage. Even questions of geography, such as, "Where does your son live?" may be a sensitive issue to a parent whose son is in jail or in a psychiatric hospital or totally out of contact with the parent. The family's initial concealment of information may often be overcome by careful, sensitive exploration of the situation.

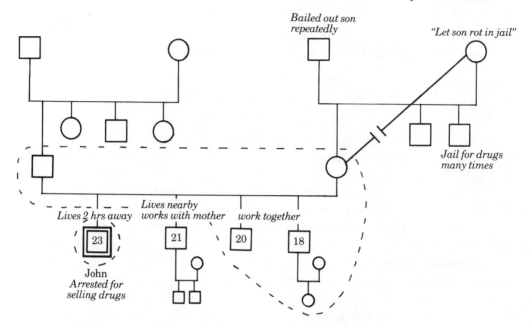

Diagram 4.1 The G. family

For example, the G.'s, an Italian/WASP family, were referred for consultation by their lawyer, who hoped the referral would influence the court case of the oldest of their three sons, John, who had been arrested for selling drugs. The genogram is shown in Diagram 4.1.

Initially the family presented a united front: They were a close, loving family whose son had come under the influence of "bad friends." They denied the seriousness of the son's crime, offered little factual information, minimized any relationship problems, but said they were willing to do anything to help. Few connections were apparent in gathering the basic genogram information until we got to the question of the whereabouts of the maternal uncle. Mrs. G. said that she did not know where her brother was, but then admitted that he was in jail and had had many previous arrests. This led to questioning about the maternal grandmother's reaction to John's problem, at which point the family's united front began to break down. The parents reluctantly admitted that they had stopped talking to the maternal grandmother since John's arrest because of her "insensitive" response: "Let him rot in jail." (Mr. and Mrs. G. had taken a second mortgage on their house to pay their son's bail and legal fees.) Mrs. G. said she had always been very close to her mother and could not understand what had happened, but said she viewed her mother as "disloyal." Further detailed questioning led to the information that Mrs. G.'s brother had first been arrested at age 23 (John's present age). The maternal grandfather had repeatedly bailed his son out of trouble, spending all the family savings on this, against the grandmother's wishes, and she was now very bitter that her son had brought almost total ruin on her family. It was only through discussing the details of the uncle's criminal behavior (a family secret that John and his brothers did not know), that the family's "cool" about their present situation was broken. Mrs. G. talked about her pain in watching her own mother's agony over the years, as well as her own fury at her brother for the shame he had brought on the family. She was desperately afraid of reliving her parents' experience, but since even discussing the matter with her mother made her more fearful that the family was "doomed" to repeat the past, she had stopped talking to her mother. As we talked, John's brothers opened up for the first time in the interview, expressing their resentment of their brother for putting the family in the terrible position of having to decide whether to put their life savings on the line or let John go to jail. The father, who had been the most adamant in denying any family difficulties, talked about his sense of betrayal and failure that his son had so cut him off. It was only through the leverage of the previous family experiences that the family's present conflicts became evident.

The genogram interview is especially useful for engaging obsessive, unresponsive or uninvolved clients. The obsessive client who otherwise dwells on the endless details of family minutiae often comes quickly to emotionally loaded and significant material during a genogram interview. Unresponsive clients often find themselves caught up in reciting and responding to the family drama.

In their attempt to avoid dealing with painful past experiences and unresolved emotional issues, families often rigidify their relationships and view of the themselves. Calm, nonthreatening, "research" questions can often open up these matters, so that family members can begin to relate to one another in a different way around such issues.

One common issue around which families become blocked is that of loss and death. Norman and Betty Paul (1974) use genograms to unblock the family system by focusing on losses in the multigenerational family. They do not treat symptoms directly, but rather involve the clients in a search for deaths or life-threatening experiences in either the immediate or extended family. In the Pauls' view, the "forgetting" and distortion in family members' perceptions that occur around loss are among the most important factors influencing symptom development. The Pauls routinely send genogram forms to prospective clients to be completed before the first session; they find that this gives them important information about how the clients orient themselves to their original family. In the first session they carefully track the dates of birth and death and the causes of death of family members for the past three generations. In their experience, clients usually indicate some degree of mystification about doing their genograms. They report an interesting example of a response to the genogram in *A Marital Puzzle* (1974). A husband was asked to bring genogram information to the first therapy session. He left off the chart the fact that both of his parents had died, although he had been specifically asked for it; when questioned, he said he did not remember exactly when they had died. The Pauls' therapeutic model involves rediscovery of such dissociated family experiences.

Clarifying Family Patterns

Clarifying family patterns is at the heart of genogram usage. As we collect information to complete the genogram, we are constantly constructing and revising hypotheses based on our ongoing understanding of the family. Then, in conjunction with other clinical data, we often present our observations to the family. We usually offer our observations as tentative hypotheses which the family may confirm or disprove.

The G. family discussed above illustrates how the genogram can become a guide for both family and therapist to patterns, clarifying the present dilemma in ways which open up possibilities for alternative behavior in the future. From the genogram, we could see a pattern of repetition of criminal behavior. Then, as the connection was made between the son's and the uncle's criminal behavior and the possibility of the family history being repeated was pointed out, the family began to look at the son's behavior within the family context and to explore the legacy and conflicts that were perpetuating the behavior.

Clarifying family patterns serves an educational function for the family, allowing family members to see their behavior as connected and within the family context. Cognitive understanding of symptomatic behavior as it relates to emotionally charged relationships can increase the family's sense of mastery over the family plight. In addition, it is often difficult to maintain dysfunctional behavior once the family patterns that underlie it are clarified.

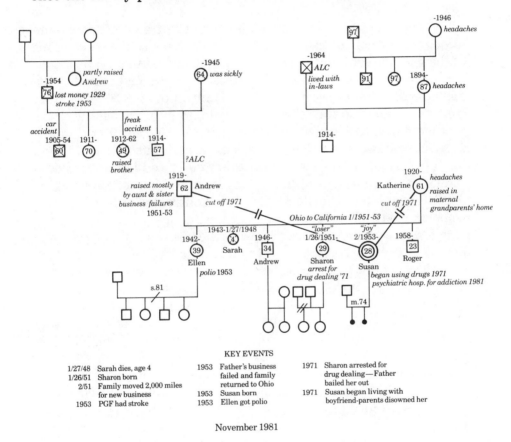

KEY EVENTS

1/27/48 Sarah dies, age 4	1953 Father's business failed and family returned to Ohio	1971 Sharon arrested for drug dealing—Father bailed her out
1/26/51 Sharon born		
2/51 Family moved 2,000 miles for new business	1953 Susan born	1971 Susan began living with boyfriend-parents disowned her
1953 PGF had stroke	1953 Ellen got polio	

November 1981

Diagram 4.2 The B. family

In the B. family a number of patterns needing clarification became apparent in the process of interpreting the genogram. Susan B. first sought help for headaches in 1971, when her parents disowned her for moving in with her boyfriend while in college. She began a long history of addiction to Valium and other prescription drugs, culminating in a hospitalization for drug abuse in 1981. The genogram (Diagram 4.2) was constructed in the first interview.

Applying the interpretive principles to the genogram reveals a number of significant clinical patterns. In terms of pattern repetition across generations (Category 3), Susan was the fourth generation of women suffering from chronic headaches. In addition, Susan's pattern of anesthetizing herself with drugs fits with her mother's pill-taking for headaches and her father's and maternal grandfather's alcohol abuse.

By tracking the coincidence and impact of significant events (Category 4), we find that Susan was born in February, a special time of the year for her family: An older sister had died five years earlier, on January 27, 1948, and another sister, Sharon, had been born on January 26, 1951, the very month the family moved 2000 miles away from their home so that the father could go into business with his brother-in-law. In addition, Susan, born in 1953, came into the family at a time following multiple crises: The father's business had failed, his brother-in-law moved in with the family, and his father had a stroke while visiting and had to move in and be nursed until his death a year later. The oldest daughter contracted polio (the sister who had died had had spinal meningitis) and had to be put in a iron lung for several months, and following the business failure, the family moved back to the Midwest to start over. A year later, father's older brother died in a car accident. Both parents are the youngest in their sibling constellation (mother's mother was also a youngest). Given the youngest's propensity to expect to be cared for by others (Category 1: family structure), one might speculate about how well they could support and care for one another during this difficult period.

Noticing all the difficulties of this period, the therapist inquired further as to its impact on the family. Mother reported that Susan was her one "joy" in the midst of everything else that was going wrong. The two surviving daughters came to play complementary roles: Susan was the "good" child while Sharon became the "loser." Interestingly, two months before Susan's cut-off from her parents, Sharon had been bailed out by her parents after having been arrested with her drug dealer husband. Seeing the patterns on the genogram, the therapist was able to explore and clarify with the family the cross-generational repetition of coping methods, the impact of critical family events, and the interconnectedness of the two sisters' behavior.

Reframing and Detoxifying Family Issues

Families develop their own particular ways of viewing themselves. In problematic families, the family's perspective is often rigid and resistant to change or to alternative views of the situation. Genograms are an important tool for reframing behavior, relationships, and time connections in the family, and for "detoxifying" and normalizing the family's perception of itself. Suggesting alternative interpretations of the family's experience points the way to new possibilities in the future.

The genogram interview allows the clinician many opportunities to normalize the family members' understanding of their situation. Simply bringing up an issue or putting it in a more normative perspective can often "detoxify" it. Using information gathered on the genogram, the clinician can also actively reframe the meaning of behavior in the family system, enabling the family members to see themselves in a different way. The interpretive guidelines indicate some of the possible ways for doing this. The family structure (Category 1) suggests normative expectations for behavior and relationships (e.g., "It's not surprising you're so responsible since oldest children commonly are." Or, "Usually two youngest who marry tend to be waiting for each other to take care of them. How did it go with you?"). Similarly, an understanding of life cycle fit (Category 2) can provide a normalizing experience (e.g., "People who marry as late as you did are usually pretty set in their ways"). Pattern repetition (Category 3) and the coincidence of events (Category 4) show the larger context of problematic behavior (e.g., "Maybe how you were feeling had something to do with all the stressful events that were occurring at the time"). And relational patterns (Category 5) and family balance (Category 6) help demonstrate the interdependency of family members (e.g., "Most people react that way as the odd person out." Or, "Usually, when one person takes on more than her share of responsibility, then the other person takes on less").

Bowen is a master at detoxifying reactive responses with genogram questioning. For example, below is an excerpt of an interview by Bowen of a man who felt intimidated by his "domineering, possessive mother":

> *Bowen:* What are the problems of being the only child of an only child mother?

Client: My mother was a very domineering woman who never wanted to let go of anything she possessed, including me.

Bowen: Well, if you're the only one, wouldn't that be sort of predictable? Often in a relationship like that people can with some accuracy know what the other thinks . . . in other words, you're describing a sort of an intense relationship, and not too unusual with a mother and an only son, especially a mother who doesn't have a husband, and your mother was an only. How would you characterize your mother's relationship with her mother?

Here Bowen is using what we would call family structure (Category 1) to normalize a mother's behavior and the special mother-child bond of an only child. Bowen's therapy is characterized throughout by such tracking, detoxifying and reframing of multigenerational family patterns.

Other Uses of the Genogram in Family Therapy

Family therapists with a Bowen systemic approach have been using genograms for many years as the primary tool for assessment and for designing therapeutic interventions. More recently, therapists with different approaches have come to use the genogram for recordkeeping, family assessment, and designing strategic interventions.

Wachtel has suggested using the genogram as a "quasi-projective technique" in family therapy, revealing unarticulated fears, wishes and values of the individuals in the family. She takes about four one-hour sessions to complete a genogram on a marital couple. After getting the basic "factual data," she asks each spouse for a list of adjectives to describe each family member, and then for stories to illustrate the adjectives used. She keeps track of the conceptions the spouses have about various family members and how these conceptions are passed down from one generation to another. She then investigates the spouses' conception of the relationships between people, commenting throughout "on emerging family issues, patterns, and assumptions and their possible relevance to the current situation" (1982, p. 342). Differences of opinion become grist for the mill of therapy, and spouses are urged to seek missing genogram information between sessions.

More recently, therapists using a strategic approach have come to use the genogram not only for recordkeeping and family assessment, but as a map for designing strategic interventions. The following example, taken from a case in which a modification of the Milan model was used, illustrates the strategic use of genogram patterns and events.

The S. family applied for help because the younger of their two daughters, Karen, age 19, had begun to binge and vomit after leaving home for college and had been losing weight. Judy, her older sister, was one year ahead of Karen at a local college. All members described their family as closer than other families, loving and open. Karen's problem was a mystery to everyone, herself included. The genogram (Diagram 4.3) was taken on the family.

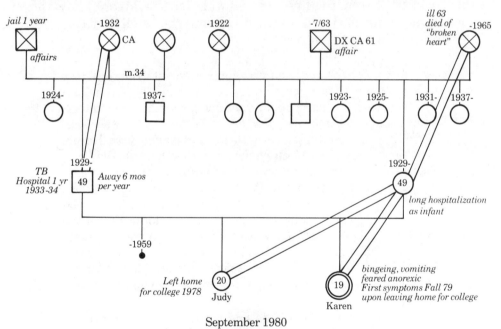

September 1980

Diagram 4.3 The S. family

The therapist used the information gathered from the genogram to "positively connote" and normalize the family's behavior and experience. The current family situation was related to the repetition of family patterns (Category 3), the impact of critical events in the family's history (Category 4), and the complementary balance of family functioning (Category 6). For example, Karen's difficulties leaving home were related to her special position in the family due to deaths of maternal grandparents shortly after her birth. The special closeness of the family was explained by the parents' early childhood experiences with loss and isolation: the mother having had a long hospitalization when 18 months old and the father losing his mother and being hospitalized at age three. The parents' fears of closeness with each other and Karen's need to protect them were also explained and justified by the early losses. And the observation of a female sisterhood both among the daughters and among the mother's siblings was used to cast a sympathetic light on the father's isolation in the family. Thus, the genogram was used to depict a positive, understanding view of the family while at the same time implying that change was possible when the family was ready for it. An excerpt from the first session will give the flavor of how the genogram information is used to reframe the family's pattern of adaptation in a positive way:

> *Therapist:* We have been very impressed with the closeness and mutual sacrifice you all show for your family. Even from the little we have heard about your background, we can understand some of the issues: For example, Mrs. S.'s father's diagnosis of cancer coincided with her pregnancy with Karen, and shortly after her birth he died and then his wife died of a "broken heart" shortly afterwards, making Karen's position in the family a very special one. Mr. S., who had very little warmth in his own family because of his mother's early death, has been forced to be away from his family half the year for work; yet the family makes great efforts to include you when you are available. Somehow, it seems to us that Karen's not eating is symbolic of the family's sacrifice for each other to maintain closeness in the face of the difficulties and losses they have experienced.

Pointing out why a family is the way it is and cannot change sometimes leads to change. Genogram patterns are used in this therapeutic model first to convey a positive understanding of the present dysfunctional situation and thus paradoxically challenge the rigidity of the present stabilization. As change does occur, genogram information is again used to reinforce emerging patterns and to underline the normative evolution of the family.

For example, as the S. family's therapy continued, various family triangles were dealt with in clinical interventions. One triangle involved the mother and daughters together with the father in the outside position. (There can be more than three people involved in a triangle. They occupy three positions: two in and one out.) During the course of therapy both Judy and Karen developed relationships with boyfriends. We then raised questions about whether these relationships would threaten the sisterhood since the daughters were demonstrating loyalty to persons outside the basic nuclear family triangle where the women, daughters and mother, were close and the father was in the outside position. This point was reinforced by pointing out that a similar triangle had existed in Mrs. S.'s family of origin, where the father was kept "on a pedestal" and always an outsider to the mother-daughter closeness. Pointing out the triangles and validating the loyalty issues seemed to add enough flexibility to the system for the daughters to maintain relationships outside the home.

GENOGRAM APPLICATIONS IN FAMILY PRACTICE

Families can be a source of both stress and support in times of medical illness. The genogram, as a primary tool for describing families and their functioning, is a crucial instrument in family health care. In the following brief discussion, we will focus on three areas: 1) systemic medical recordkeeping, 2) rapport-building, and 3) medical management and preventive medicine.

Systemic Medical Recordkeeping

Family physicians and other health care personnel with a commitment to continuing comprehensive care assume the responsibility of treating individuals not alone but in the context of their families (Litman, 1974; Richardson, 1945). There is, moreover, growing research evidence of the relationship between the level of family functioning and the physical and emotional well-being of each family member (Lewis et al., 1976; Schmidt, 1978). The illness of an individual family member will disrupt the family's functioning; on the other hand, family dynamics may have a role in the development of illness in family members (Doherty & Baird, 1983). For example, family stresses have been related to the occurrence of a variety of illnesses (Haggerty & Albert, 1967) and to the severity and duration of respiratory illnesses in children (Boyce et al., 1977). In addition, the importance of family supports in counteracting such stresses

(Caplan, 1976; Cobb, 1976; Massad, 1980) and the role of family functioning in adherence and clinical response to treatment regimens (Steidl et al., 1980) have been demonstrated. In other words, the relationship between the family and the patient is a major factor in the development and outcome of an illness.

Thus, it makes sense for health care providers to gather family information relevant to understanding medical problems in their systemic family context. Unfortunately, however, most physicians do not pay systematic attention to family patterns, because they have no way to keep track of them and they have not been taught how to make use of family information in the limited time they have available.

The genogram is perhaps the most clinically useful tool so far developed for assessing these connections between the family and illness. It is both efficient and economical since it enables the physician to gather quickly specifically relevant information on the family and to record the information in a clear, easily readable format.

The major advantage of the genogram is its graphic format. When there is a genogram in the medical record, the clinician can glance at it and get an immediate picture of the family and medical situation without wading through a stack of notes. Critical medical information can be flagged on the genogram and the current medical problem can be seen immediately in its larger familial and historical context. Thus, the genogram in itself enhances a systemic perspective of illness.

Genograms can be gathered in a medical setting in a number of ways. Patients can complete a form before their first visit (see Appendix, Part 3). Or a technician, nurse, secretary or medical student can take a genogram before the patient sees the physician for the first visit. Such genograms can be collected in 15–20 minutes even by a relatively unskilled interviewer. Or the physician can take the genogram, either at the first interview or as part of the patient's comprehensive medical history interview. Practically, however, due to time limitations, the physician may be able to gather only very basic information in the first interview; details can be added to the genogram as a relationship develops with the patient.

Rapport-building

The process of gathering family information with the genogram may contribute to the establishment of rapport between the clinician and the patient. Interestingly, Rogers and Durkin (1984) found that most patients, after being given a 20-minute genogram interview, felt that such an interview could improve their medical care and their communication with their physicians. In an increasingly complex, technological, fast-paced medical world, patients sometimes complain of impersonal medical technologists who show interest only in their disorders, rather than in them as people. Genogram interviewing shows an interest in the well-being of each family member. This can be particularly important since medical compliance is so often related to the family's confidence and trust in the physician and other medical personnel.

Medical Management and Preventive Medicine

Finally, there is the application of the genogram in the management of medical treatment. Family physicians can and sometimes do use their knowledge of patients' family relationships and patterns to develop diagnostic and therapeutic plans for their patients (Anstett & Collins, 1982; Christie-Seely, 1981; Fossom et al., 1982; Rosen et al., 1982). The information on the genogram may be used directly in treatment planning or as a basis for referral.

Smilkstein (1984) has recently argued that an assessment of family functioning is relevant to medical treatment in that: 1) the physician may be able to "anticipate illness behavior, and in some instances to initiate preventive measures"; 2) such an assessment "can be beneficial in anticipating compliance" and evaluating available resources for aiding in compliance; 3) documenting life events may pinpoint stressors that may affect treatment; and 4) critical psychosocial problems may call for active intervention and/or outside referral. He suggests that it is particularly in "patient problem areas such as somatization, high utilization, multiple complaints, and chronic pain that assessment of family functioning and social support in general will be most rewarding" (pp. 266–7).

The genogram as an assessment instrument may serve all of the above functions. Indications on the genogram of previous illnesses or symptom patterns may lead to early detection of a problem and preventive treatment of family members at risk. The relational patterns on a genogram may suggest the likelihood of a family's complying with a given treatment recommendation and indicate what social supports will be available for managing an illness. The genogram shows the critical life events that may be stressing a patient, both currently and historically. Such events suggest a reorganization of the family to adapt to the change, particularly when life cycle transitions or role changes are involved. And finally, the genogram is an important record of the psychosocial functioning of the family that may indicate when intervention is necessary.

Following are two examples of how a genogram may be used in medical treatment.

The first example illustrates the importance of gathering information in the initial interview. A 28-year-old chemical engineer sought help at a local family practice center for stomach pains in August 1984. Because it was customary for the nurse to take a genogram on new patients prior to the doctor-patient encounter, Diagram 4.4 was drawn.

Working from the genogram, the doctor began by trying to put the patient's stomach pain in context. She noted that this was a particularly difficult time for Mr. A. and hypothesized that recent critical family events might have had a stressful impact on him and his family (Category 4, life events and family functioning). The patient and his wife of one and a half years were in the midst of several major transitions. They had moved six months earlier and they were expecting their first child in five months. In addition, the patient's sister and her husband had recently separated, an event whose impact might be reverberating throughout the family system.

Looking carefully at the genogram we notice a number of temporal connections, anniversary reactions, and repetitive patterns that might be exacerbating the stressful nature of the upcoming events for Mr. A. His first wife had died of cancer in August 1981, which might well make this time of year particularly painful for him (Category 4, anniversary reaction). There is a repetitive pattern of early female death: His mother, his maternal grandmother, and his first wife all died in their twenties, which might make him acutely sensitive to physical vulnerability of women in his family (Category 3, multigenerational patterns). It thus seemed likely to the physician that Mr. A. would be particularly worried about his wife's upcoming childbirth, especially since his maternal grandmother had died in childbirth and his sister had had two miscarriages before her recent separation.

Since Mr. A. and his mother occupied similar sibling positions on the genogram (both were youngests), the physician speculated that

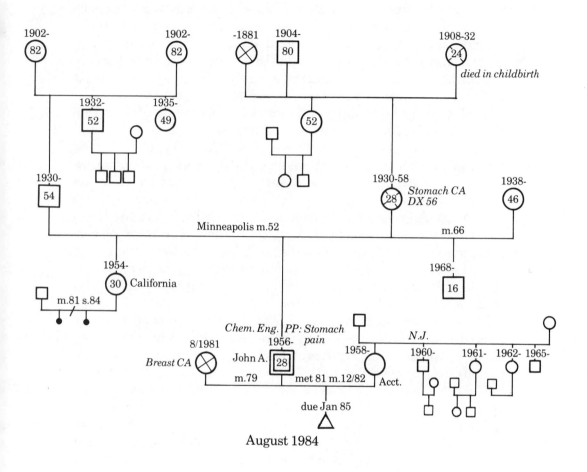

Diagram 4.4 The A. family

Mr. A. might have identified with his mother (Category 3, repeated structural patterns) and might now fear dying himself, since he was the same age as his mother when she died (Category 4, coincidence of life events).

The physician also noted the timing of the couple's marriage (Category 2, life cycle fit). Mr. A. met his current wife a week after his first wife's funeral and they were married within a year. Given the short transition period, the physician wondered whether Mr. A. had resolved his relationship with his first wife and hypothesized a hidden triangle in which the present wife was in some ways the outsider to the unresolved relationship with his first wife (Category 5, triangles in remarried families).

And finally, looking at the level of support in the family, it was evident that Mr. A. had no family in the area, while his wife's parents and all her siblings were nearby, which, perhaps, left the couple with an imbalance in emotional resources (Category 6).

During a brief discussion of these family factors, Mr. A. was able to admit his fears about the pregnancy, as well as continuing thoughts of his first wife, about which he felt guilty. He accepted a referral for consultation with a family therapist. Physical examination did indicate that Mr. A. was suffering from gastroesophageal reflux, probably exacerbated by his emotional state. Medication was prescribed. The patient was requested to bring his wife along to his follow-up visit two weeks later. At that time he had gone for the consultation with the family therapist and his symptoms had disappeared. He and his wife were apparently doing a good deal of talking about his past experiences and he was feeling much better psychologically as well as physically.

The genogram interview had identified the psychosocial stressors that needed to be dealt with and the referral had begun the process, easing the pressure for Mr. A. and his family. The genogram allowed the physician the opportunity to practice preventive medicine.

The next example illustrates a more complex case, in which the response to genogram information was less immediate. Dan R. went to see his physician complaining of heart palpitations. The doctor learned that his father had died of a heart attack and his mother of multiple heart attacks and strokes, but could find no evidence of an organic problem. He decided that he needed to find out more about Mr. R.'s family history and obtained the genogram shown in Diagram 4.5.

The doctor noted from the genogram a number of family events that might be affecting Mr. R. (Category 4, life events and family functioning). His son, John, who had had many behavioral and drug problems before joining the service, was due to return home shortly, and perhaps Mr. R. was worried about the problems starting again. His ex-wife's mother had recently died, which might lead to his ex-wife's putting more pressure on him because of her own grief and anxiety. Mr. R. had a sister who was continuing to deteriorate from multiple sclerosis. As the oldest in the family, and with his parents no longer alive, he was likely feeling responsible for his sister's care (Category 1, sibling constellation), particularly as his brother had died of the same disease. He might also fear his own genetic vulnerability to the disease.

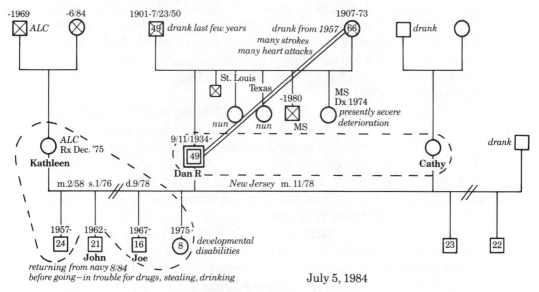

Diagram 4.5 The R. family

Also of interest to the family physician was the potential repetition of a structural pattern (Category 3) and the patient's possible anniversary reaction (Category 4). Mr. R. was now the same age as his father when he had died of a heart attack, and Mr. R.'s youngest son, Joe, was 16, the age he had been at the time his father died. Perhaps Mr. R. feared that history would repeat itself and the heart palpitations were an expression of this anxiety.

Finally, there was the pattern repetition (Category 3) of drinking in the family. Both of his parents had had drinking problems, as did his son, his first wife, and the families of both of his wives. Based on this history, it was possible that Mr. R. had a drinking problem or that his family thought he did.

Based on the genogram information, the physician was able to ask Mr. R. about each of these areas of concern: his son coming home, his ex-wife, his debilitated sister, his being the same age as his father when he died, and the drinking. While Mr. R. admitted to some general concern in each of these areas except drinking, he

was sure they had no bearing on his physical state, saying he never
let things like that get to him. As for the drinking, he said his wife
thought he drank too much, but that was just because her father
and her first husband were alcoholics and she was too sensitive. This
answer, of course, raised more questions about the extent and nature
of his drinking and about his relationship with his wife. Although
physical findings were negative, the physician decided, on the basis
of the information gathered here and the patient's response, to request a follow-up visit with both Mr. and Mrs. R. two weeks later,
"just to see how the heart was doing."

At the follow-up meeting the family stresses were reviewed and
Mrs. R. confirmed her worries about her husband's anxiety and
drinking. The doctor mentioned the possibility of their going to AA
or Al-Anon or to therapy, but the idea was immediately rejected by
both spouses. However, a month later Mrs. R. called back, saying
that she felt the tension had not diminished and she would now like
the name of a therapist they could consult. The doctor again suggested that she could attend Al-Anon, but she refused, although she
did take the name of a local therapist. At medical follow-up six
months later, Mr. R. proudly announced that he had celebrated his
50th birthday and felt very relieved and healthy. He said he had been
trying to deal with his ex-wife about their son John, who seemed
not to be getting on his feet after leaving the navy and was drinking too much.

Although neither Mr. R. nor his wife responded immediately to
the doctor's observations about the family situation, the genogram
did help him to assess the family stress and relationship factors and
gradually to become an important resource for the spouses at the
point when they could respond. They will undoubtedly need to turn
to him again in the future, and having the genogram in the chart
will make it easier for him to keep track of ongoing changes as the
children develop, as Mr. R.'s sister's condition gets worse, as his conflicts with his ex-wife abate or continue, and if tension with his present wife over alcohol resurfaces.

There are indications that when one member of a family is in dis-
tress, others will react as well (Huygen, 1982; Widmer et al., 1980).
In this case, by recognizing the multiple stresses Mr. R. was experiencing, the physician became aware of the need to bring in Mrs.
R. as well, to evaluate her response and ability to support her husband, and to at least plant the seed that other help was available

for them if they should want to use it. This probably made it easier for Mrs. R. to seek the referral when she did, since her doctor was already familiar with the situation and had himself suggested a source of help for them.

In sum, genograms used in medical practice can suggest what family patterns are repeating themselves, so that preventive measures can be taken; what resources the patient has to help with an illness; what problems there may be in medical compliance; what family stresses may be intensifying the difficulty; and what type of further psychosocial intervention is needed, such as including others in follow-up medical visits or making outside referrals.

5

THE FUTURE OF
THE GENOGRAM

One of the most exciting possibilities of the genogram is its potential for further research on families and family process. Since so many clinicians already collect family information on genograms, we feel that these practical, everyday clinical genograms are too valuable a research resource to ignore.

Although the genogram is almost as old as the field of family therapy, there has been little systematic development of the genogram as an instrument for either assessment or research. In fact, as far as we know, this book represents the first attempt to spell out the principles for interpreting the genogram. There is a great deal of work yet to be done. Three areas are especially promising: 1) research on the genogram as a clinical tool; 2) research on families and family process using the genogram for assessment; and 3) computer-generated genograms.

It is our view that the genogram has a tremendous potential both clinically and in research on families and family process because it is a relatively simple, non-intrusive, easily updated tool for collecting current and historical family information, already used routinely by many clinicians. The pooling and computerization of these genograms could provide an extensive data-base for family research. Since the genogram is relevant to clinical work, the clinician as data collector is motivated to gather accurate, meaningful information. Thus, the usual problem of obtaining cooperation from on-line clinicians for research is partly avoided.

RESEARCH ON THE GENOGRAM AS A CLINICAL TOOL

The genogram has been used by clinicians as a format for collecting, organizing, and interpreting data, rather than as a standardized measurement technique. Hence, family clinicians have not been particularly concerned with the psychometric characteristics of the genogram, or even with reliability and validity in the usual sense of those terms. Nevertheless, we believe the usefulness of the genogram to clinical practice can and should be demonstrated. Work is needed to show that the genogram is relatively reliable and accurate, i.e., the information gathered is consistent over time, across different members of the family, and when different interviewers collect the information. There are a number of factors that may affect the reliability of genogram information. First of all, some data are more inferential than other data, e.g., demographic information such as names and dates is more objective than judgments of functioning or relationship. Second, the information collected is often subject to distortions resulting from the theoretical biases of different clinicians. Third, there is the fallibility of human memory, particularly for stressful life events. And finally, there is the phenomenon of different perspectives on the same event (the *Rashomon* effect). Clearly, members of the same family do not always agree in their reports of emotionally significant events. In fact, as mentioned in Chapter 2, forgetfulness and discrepancies in reporting of dates or events by different family members offer important clues to unacknowledged emotionally significant issues in the family.

Although there has been little actual empirical research on the reliability of the genogram, Jolly, Froom, and Rosen (1980) found that family practice residents could elicit and record most of the "relevant" family information during a 16-minute genogram interview and the information thus gathered could be read correctly from the genogram by different physicians with a high degree of accuracy. The sample was small and homogeneous and the "relevant" data were limited to objective information sought by physicians; nevertheless, the findings suggest the strong potential of the genogram as a recording tool.

We are also interested in how genograms are put to clinical use. It would be important to demonstrate, for example, that clinicians who use genograms are able to develop better, or at least different, predictions about families than those who do not. We would be particularly interested in whether other experienced clinicians use interpretive categories and principles similar to those outlined in Chapter 3. Of course, it would also be important to assess whether the predictions made using the genogram are accurate and whether the conclusions derived from a genogram interview correlate with other family assessment instruments.

In the end, the proof of the value of the genogram will be a documentation of its impact on clinical practice. First of all, research on the genogram is necessary to establish whether families that participate in genogram interviews benefit in some way from their involvement. In a recent study, patients who gave family history information in a brief genogram interview reported later that they felt the genogram would help their physician understand them better and thus provide improved health care (Rogers & Durkin, 1984). In family therapy, one could study the effects of a genogram interview on the joining process or attitudes toward therapy. One might ask whether this form of assessment actually helps family members to "think systemically," to see their problems as "making sense" within a broader life context, and as being more manageable.

Equally important, research on the genogram should address the benefits of the genogram for the clinician. Does the use of the genogram lead to richer, more helpful formulations of the family problem? Does the genogram actually make a difference in how clinicians intervene? Does it help clinicians to think more systemically? For example, would the routine use of the genogram make physicians more sensitive to broader psychosocial issues that may affect health care? Such research will establish the clinical relevance of the genogram and determine its long-term use in clinical practice.

RESEARCH ON FAMILIES AND FAMILY PROCESS

A number of steps need to be taken to adapt the genogram for empirical research on families. The conditions under which it is a reliable assessment instrument must be established. A standardized genogram format and interview protocol should be used in such genogram research. We hope that the conventions for constructing a genogram and interviewing families presented in this book will help in this direction. Clear standards for constructing genograms, proper training, and possibly the computerization of the process will all lead to more reliable data from the genogram.

Research on families using the genogram would involve testing the basic assumptions about family processes that guide the way genograms are used by clinicians. Many of these assumptions are based on Bowen's family systems theory and are quite testable. To give a flavor of this type of research, we will use our categories of interpretive principles as a framework for suggesting just a few of the many possible researchable questions.

Family structure: Is symptomatology seen in some family structures more often than in others? Is sibling position related to achievement motivation, responsibility or symptomatology? Are couples with complementary sibling positions (oldest and youngest) more compatible than couples with non-complementary sibling positions (both oldest or both youngest)?

Life cycle fit: Are families more likely to become symptomatic at points of life cycle transition? What are the normative ages for passing through each phase of the family life cycle? Is there disturbance in the system when life cycle transitions are unduly rushed or delayed? Do couples who marry early or late or who are at different points in their own life cycles have particular types of problems?

Pattern repetition across generations: What symptoms and problems are likely to be passed down from one generation to another? How common are alternating repetitive patterns of cut-off and fusion and high and low functioning? Can levels of "maturity" or differentiation be tracked from one generation to another?

Life events and family functioning: Do traumatic or critical family events occur around certain dates at a greater than chance frequency? Is there a greater chance of symptomatology and/or "specialness" for children born around nodal events in families? What impact do untimely deaths have on other family members?

Relational patterns and triangles: Are there typical types of relational patterns that correspond to particular family structures (e.g., child-focused families, remarried families)? How do triangles in families change over time? How does a particular child get selected to be included in a parental-child triangle and thus become symptomatic?

Family balance and imbalance: Is there a balance in functioning in families across generations? What happens when there is an imbalance or lack of functional fit in a family? How does functional balance shift in families, e.g., under what conditions does a dysfunctional spouse become functional while the reverse occurs with the other spouse?

Many of the above questions could be researched simply by analyzing objective data across a large number of genograms. To do this, however, the data must be pooled together and organized, most likely through the use of a computer.

COMPUTER-GENERATED GENOGRAMS

Imagine a clinician sitting down at a computer, entering some information on a family, and, presto, a genogram appears on the screen. Or imagine the same clinician reviewing his or her previous caseload and wondering how effective he or she might be with families with small children. The computer is told to search for this type of family and the relevant family genograms one by one appear on the screen or are printed out. Or finally, imagine the clinician wondering if there might be a pattern to a series of families he or she has seen. Again, the computer is consulted and asked to search for certain hypothesized features in each of the relevant families. This may seem like science fiction, but with computer technology developing at an amazing pace, the day is not far off when the computer might become an invaluable part of the clinician's armamentarium.

At the very least, the computer may take over one of the more mechanical tasks in family assessment: constructing the genogram. The computer can take the spatial guesswork out of drawing genograms and easily update and redraw a genogram as new information on the family is gathered. The computer, however, will be more helpful than simply a genogram drawer. The computer is an information manager. It can organize and retrieve information efficiently and quickly. Equally important, the computer can present information in a variety of forms and can be instructed to search for redundancies and patterns in data. All of these abilities may be useful in assessing and studying families.

The value of the computer for large-scale genogram research is obvious. We have already mentioned the tremendous untapped data pool present in the thousands of genograms produced daily by clinicians. This information could only become useful for research if it became part of a computer data-base. Our hope is that as clinicians begin to use computers to store and generate their genograms, the pooling of the individual clinician's computer data on families (with identifying information omitted) will lead to a very large data-base for research purposes.

Over the past three years Gerson (1984) has developed a computer program for generating genograms on an Apple II computer. Although still in a rudimentary stage of development, the program can already draw three-generational genograms based on family information entered into the computer. The computer eliminates the usual design problems of creating a neat, well-spaced, readable genogram. When new information is entered, the program changes the genogram for the therapist automatically. In fact, this program developed out of the frustration of having to redraw genograms whenever significant new information was gained about a family member. From the computer-generated genogram, the clinician can access information on each individual family member. In addition, the program can produce genograms for any date in the family's history. Thus, if the clinician chooses to show the family ten years earlier, the computer will display the corresponding age of each family member at that time and eliminate family members who were not yet born. Also, the computer can compile a comprehensive chronology of important family events. Finally, the program allows the clinician to specify critical family relationships as fused, distant, etc., and the corresponding relationship lines appear on the genogram.

This program is a first step in the evolution of computerized family information systems which we believe will be of great use to family clinicians and researchers. Our goal is to develop a practical method of computerizing family information that emphasizes a systemic view of the family.

A major trend toward the automation of clinical records has occurred in recent years. When such records are placed in a computer data-base, the information is more accessible and usable. Different clinicians can easily have access to the same files and information. In addition, automatic flags can be set up to warn the clinician of conditions applying in specific cases, e.g., a review due on a certain date. The computer-generated genogram is an obvious application of family systems thinking to the collection of family information. However, efforts in this direction are just beginning. As computer technology advances, the potential of the computer in the organization and display of data will change as well. We are beginning to explore the potential of other computers with more advanced graphic capabilities to see how suited they may be to schematizing family information.

One day, family members themselves may sit down at a computer and enter information about their families. The clinician may want to display computer-generated genograms to make specific systemic points. The computer could become a part of the therapeutic process. We do not fear that the machine will replace the human. Human judgment and intervention will always remain central to clinical work. However, the machine may become an important partner in information management and organization.

The information managing capabilities of computers are too awesome to simply ignore. The hope is to make those capabilities of direct use to the clinician and researcher. The computer-generated genogram is an example of such an application which organizes family information in a graphic form to emphasize the systemic, multigenerational nature of the family.

In conclusion, we have strived in this book to show the usefulness of genograms in clinical work. Our hope is that our preliminary efforts will serve as guide to the further development of the genogram as both a clinical and research tool. We believe that the research potential of the genogram has barely been touched. We see the development of the genogram as a research tool and the computerization of the genogram as going hand in hand, both leading to increased clinical proficiency and knowledge.

APPENDIX

This appendix, included for the convenience of teachers and clinicians, provides summaries of some important materials and skeletal formats for doing genograms. It includes:

1) a summary of the symbol standardization for doing genograms;
2) a skeletal genogram form for clinician use;
3) an outline for conducting a genogram interview;
4) a summary of the interpretive categories for genograms.

PART 1: GENOGRAM FORMAT

A. Symbols to describe basic family membership and structure (include on genogram significant others who lived with or cared for family members – place them on the right side of the genogram with a notation about who they are.)

Male: ☐   Female: ◯   Birth date ⟶ 43-75 ⟵ Death date

⊠
Death=X

Index Person (IP): ☐ ◯

Marriage (give date)
(Husband on left, wife on right): ☐—m.60—◯   Living together relationship or liaison: ☐ 72 ◯

Marital separation (give date): ☐ s.70 ◯   Divorce (give date): ☐ d.72 ◯

Children: List in birth order, beginning with oldest on left: 60 62 65   Adopted or foster children:

Fraternal twins: Identical twins: Pregnancy: △

3 mos.

Spontaneous abortion: ●   Induced abortion: ✕   Stillbirth: ⊠

Members of current IP household (circle them):

Where changes in custody have occurred, please note:

B. Family interaction patterns. The following symbols are optional. The clinician may prefer to note them on a separate sheet. They are among the least precise information on the genogram, but may be key indicators of relationship patterns the clinician wants to remember:

Very close relationship:

Conflictual relationship:

Distant relationship:

Estrangement or cut off
(give dates if possible):

Cut off
62–78

Fused and conflictual:

C. Medical history. Since the genogram is meant to be an orienting map of the family, there is room to indicate only the most important factors. Thus, list only major or chronic illnesses and problems. Include dates in parentheses where feasible or applicable. Use DSM-III categories or recognized abbreviations where available (e.g., cancer: CA; stroke: CVA).

D. Other family information of special importance may also be noted on the genogram:

    1) Ethnic background and migration date
    2) Religion or religious change
    3) Education
    4) Occupation or unemployment
    5) Military service
    6) Retirement
    7) Trouble with law
    8) Physical abuse or incest
    9) Obesity
    10) Smoking
    11) Dates when family members left home: LH '74.
    12) Current location of family members

    It is useful to have a space at the bottom of the genogram for notes on *other key information*: This would include critical events, changes in the family structure since the genogram was made, hypotheses and other notations of major family issues or changes. These notations should always be dated, and should be kept to a minimum, since every extra piece of information on a genogram complicates it and therefore diminishes its readability.

PART 2: GENOGRAM FORM

FAMILY NAME

Date Filled In

Filled In By

Family Address

Key Hypotheses &
Life Events

Significant Others

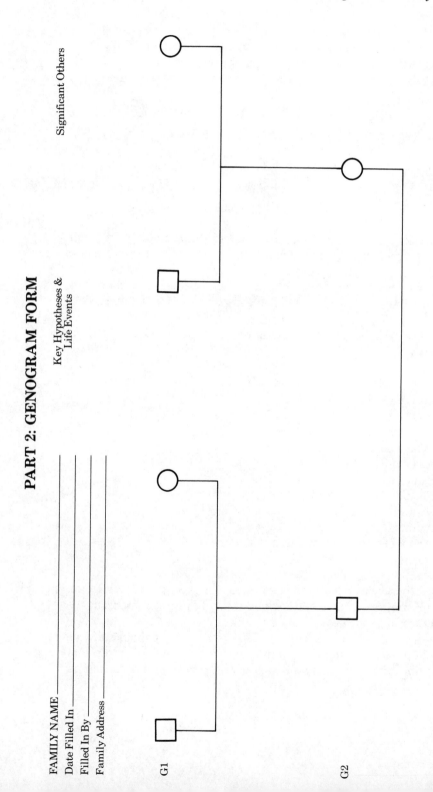

G1

G2

G3 (IP)

PART 3: OUTLINE FOR A
BRIEF GENOGRAM INTERVIEW

Index Person, Children and Spouses

Name? Date of birth? Occupation? Are they *married?* If so, give *names of spouses*, and the *name* and *sex* of *children* with each spouse. Include all *miscarriages, stillbirths, adopted* and *foster children*. Include *dates* of *marriages, separations*, and *divorces*. Also include *birth* and *death dates, cause of death, occupations* and *education* of the above family members. Who lives in *the household now?*

Family of Origin

Mother's name? *Father's* name? They were which of how many children? Give *name* and *sex* of *each sibling*. Include all *miscarriages, stillbirths, adopted* and *foster siblings*. Include *dates* of the *parents' marriages, separations*, and *divorces*. Also, include *birth* and *death dates, cause of death, occupations* and *education* of the above family members. Who lived in *the household when they were growing up?*

Mother's Family

The names of the *mother's parents?* The mother was which of how many children? Give *name* and *sex* of *each of her siblings*. Include all *miscarriages, stillbirths, adopted* and *foster siblings*. Include *dates* of *grandparents' marriages, separations*, and *divorces*. Also include *birth* and *death dates, cause of death, occupations* and *education* of the above family members.

Father's Family

The names of the *father's parents?* The father was which of how many children? Give *name* and *sex* of *each of his siblings*. Include all *miscarriages, stillbirths, adopted* and *foster siblings*. Include *dates* of *grandparents' marriages, separations*, and *divorces*. Also include *birth* and *death dates, cause of death, occupations* and *education* of the above family members.

Ethnicity

Give ethnic/religious background of family members and the languages they spoke if not English.

Major Moves

Tell about major family moves and migrations.

Significant Others

Add others who lived with or were important to the family.

For All Those Listed, Indicate Any of the Following:

serious medical, behavioral, or emotional problems;
job problems;
drug or alcohol problems;
serious problems with the law.

For All Those Listed, Indicate Any Who Were:

especially close;
distant or conflictual;
cut off from each other;
overly dependent on each other.

PART 4: GENOGRAM INTERPRETIVE CATEGORIES

Category 1: Family Structure

    A. Household composition
        1. Intact nuclear household
        2. Single-parent household
        3. Remarried family households
        4. Three-generational household
        5. Household including non-nuclear family members
    B. Sibling constellation
        1. Birth order
        2. Siblings' gender
        3. Distance in age between siblings
        4. Other factors influencing sibling constellation
            a. Timing of each child's birth in family's history
            b. Child's characteristics
            c. Family's "program" for the child
            d. Parental attitudes and biases regarding sex differences
            e. Child's sibling position in relation to that of parent
    C. Unusual family configurations

Category 2: Life Cycle Fit

Category 3: Pattern Repetition Across Generations

    A. Patterns of functioning
    B. Patterns of relationship
    C. Repeated structural patterns

Category 4: Life Events and Family Functioning

    A. Coincidences of life events
    B. The impact of life changes, transitions, and traumas
    C. Anniversary reactions
    D. Social, economic, and political events

Category 5: Relational Patterns and Triangles

    A. Triangles
    B. Parent-child triangles

    C. Common couple triangles
    D. Divorce and remarried family triangles
    E. Triangles in families with foster/adopted children
    F. Multigenerational triangles
    G. Relationships outside the family

Category 6: Family Balance and Imbalance

    A. Family structure
    B. Roles
    C. Level and style of functioning
    D. Resources

REFERENCES

(The references have been divided into two sections. The first section includes references to the professional literature on genograms and family dynamics cited in the text. The second section includes biographical sources and is arranged alphabetically by family name.)

Adler, A. (1958). *What life should mean to you?* New York: Capricorn Books.

Anstett, R. & Collins, M. (1982). The psychological significance of somatic complaints. *Journal of Family Practice, 14,* 253.

Bank, S. P. & Kahn, M. D. (1982). *The sibling bond.* New York: Basic Books.

Bepko, C. S. & Krestan, J. (1985). *The responsibility trap: Women and men in alcoholic families.* New York: The Free Press.

Booth, A. & Edwards, J. N. (1985). Age at marriage and marital instability. *Journal of Marriage and the Family, 47*(1), 67–76.

Bowen, M. (1976). Family reaction to death. In P. J. Guerin (Ed.), *Family therapy: Theory and Practice.* New York: Gardner Press.

Bowen, M. (1978). *Family therapy in clinical practice.* New York: Jason Aronson.

Bowen, M. (1980). Key to the use of the genogram. In E. A. Carter & M. McGoldrick (Eds.), *The family life cycle: A framework for family therapy.* New York: Gardner Press.

Boyce, T., Jensen, E., Cassel, J., Collier, A., Smith, A., & Ramey, C. (1977). The influence of life events and family routines on childhood respiratory tract infections. *Pediatrics, 60,* 609.

Bradt, J. (1980). *The family diagram.* Washington, D.C.: Groome Center, 5225 Loughboro Road.

Broverman, I. K., Vogel, S. R., & Broverman, D. M. (1972). Sex-role stereotypes: A current appraisal. *Journal of Social Issues, 28*(2), 59–78.

Cain, A. C. (1972). *Survivors of suicide.* Springfield, IL: Charles C Thomas.

Caplan, G. (1976). The family as a support system. In G. Caplan & H. Killelea (Eds.), *Support systems and mental health.* New York: Grune & Stratton.

Caplow, T. (1968). *Two against one: Coalitions in triads.* Englewood Cliffs, NJ: Prentice Hall.

Carter, E. A. (1978). Transgenerational scripts and nuclear family stress: Theory and clinical implications. In R. R. Sager (Ed.), *Georgetown family symposium, Vol. III (1975–76).* Washington, D.C.: Georgetown University.

Carter, E. A. (1982). Supervisory discussion in the presence of the family. In R. Whiffen & J. Byng-Hall (Eds.), *Family therapy supervision.* London: Academic Press.

Carter, E. A. & McGoldrick, M. (Eds.). (1980). *The family life cycle: A framework for family therapy.* New York: Gardner Press.

Carter, E. A., & McGoldrick Orfanidis, M. (1976). Family therapy with one person and the therapist's own family. In P. J. Guerin (Ed.), *Family therapy.* New York: Gardner Press.

Christie-Seely, J. (1981). Teaching the family system concept in family medicine. *Journal of Family Practice, 13,* 391.

Cobb, S. (1976). Social support as a moderator of life stress. *Psychosomatic Medicine, 38,* 300-314.

Doherty, W. J., & Baird, M. A. (1983). *Family therapy and family medicine.* New York: Guilford Press.

Ehrlich, R. (1976). *Mothers: 100 mothers of the famous and the infamous.* New York: Paddington Press Ltd., Two Continents Publishing Group.

Elder, G. H., Jr. (1977). Family history and the life course. *Journal of Family History, 2,* 279-304.

Engel, G. (1975). The death of a twin: Mourning and anniversary reactions: Fragments of 10 years of self-analysis. *International Journal of Psychoanalysis, 56*(1), 23-40.

Engel, G. (1980). The clinical application of the biopsychosocial model. *American Journal of Psychiatry, 137*(5), 535-544.

Entwisle, D. R., & Doering, S. G. (1981). *The first birth.* Baltimore: Johns Hopkins Press.

Ernst, C. & Angst, J. (1983). *Birth order: Its influence on personality.* New York: Springer Verlag.

Falbo, T. (Ed.). (1984). *The single-child family.* New York: Guilford Press.

Fogarty, T. (1973). Triangles. *The Family.* New Rochelle, NY: Center for Family Learning.

Forer, L. (1976). *The birth order factor.* New York: Simon & Schuster.

Fossum, A. R., Elam, C. L., & Broaddus, D. A. (1982). Family therapy in family practice: A solution to psychosocial problems? *Journal of Family Practice, 15,* 461.

Friedman, E. H. (1980). Systems and ceremonies. In E. A. Carter & M. McGoldrick (Eds.), *The family life cycle: A framework for family therapy.* New York: Gardner Press.

Friedman, E. H. (1985). *Generation to generation: Family process in church and synagogue.* New York: Guilford Press.

Garcia Preto, N. (1982). Puerto Rican families. In M. McGoldrick, J. K. Pearce, & J. Giordano (Eds.), *Ethnicity and family therapy.* New York: Guilford Press.

Gerson, R. (Oct. 1983). Computers in family therapy: Practical applications. Workshop at the annual conference of the American Association for Marital and Family Therapy, Washington, D.C.

Gerson, R. (1984). *The family recorder: computer-generated genograms.* Atlanta: Humanware Software, 61 8th St., 30327.

Gerson, R. (1985). Teaching systems psychotherapy with micro-computers. In Charles R. Figley (Ed.), *Computers and family therapy.* New York: Haworth Press.

Gerson, R. & McGoldrick, M. (in press). Genograms gathered and displayed by the computer. In John Zimmer (Ed.), *Clinics of primary care: Computers in family medicine.* Philadelphia: W. B. Saunders Co.

Glick, P. C. (1984). Marriage, divorce and living arrangements: Prospective changes. *Journal of Social Issues, 5*(7), 179-91.

Guerin, P. J. (Ed.). (1976). *Family therapy.* New York: Gardner Press.

Guerin, P. J., & Pendagast, E. G. (1976). Evaluation of family system and genogram. In P. J. Guerin (Ed.), *Family therapy.* New York: Gardner Press.

Hadley, T., Jacob, T., Miliones, J., Caplan, J., & Spitz, D. (1974). The relationship between family developmental crises and the appearance of symptoms in a family member. *Family Process, 13,* 207-14.

Haggerty, R., & Albert, J. (1967). The child, his family and illness. *Postgraduate Medicine, 34,* 228.

Haley, J. (1976). *Problem-solving therapy.* San Francisco: Jossey-Bass.

Hartman, A. (1978). Diagramatic assessment of family relationships. *Social Casework, 59,* 465-76.

Hennig, M. & Jardim, A. (1977). *The managerial woman.* Garden City: Anchor/Doubleday.

Herz, F. (1980). The impact of death and serious illness on the family life cycle. In E. A. Carter & M. McGoldrick (Eds.), *The family life cycle: A framework for family therapy.* New York: Gardner Press.

Hoffman, L. (1981). *Foundations of family therapy.* New York: Basic Books.

Holmes, T. H., & Masuda, M. (1974). Life change and illness susceptibility. In B. S. Dohrenwend & B. Dohrenwend (Eds.), *Stressful life events: Their nature and effects.* New York: John Wiley & Sons.

Holmes, T. H., and Rahe, R. H. (1967). The social adjustment rating scale. *Journal of Psycho-*

somatic Research, 11, 213–18.

Huygen, F. J. A. (1982). *Family medicine.* New York: Brunner/Mazel.

Jacobus, J. *The one child.* Manuscript in preparation.

Jolly, W. M., Froom, J., & Rosen, M. G. (1980). The genogram. *Journal of Family Practice, 10*(2), 251–255.

Kuhn, J. (1981). Realignment of emotional forces following loss. *The Family, 5*(1), 19–24.

Lewis, J. M., Beavers, W. R., Gossett, J. T., & Phillips, V. A. (1976). *No single thread: Psychological health in family systems.* New York: Brunner/Mazel.

Lieberman, S. (1979). *Transgenerational family therapy.* London: Croom Helm.

Litman, T. J. (1974). The family as a basic unit of health and medical care: A social behavioral overview. *Social Science and Medicine, 8,* 495.

Madanes, C. (1981). *Strategic family therapy.* San Francisco: Jossey-Bass.

Massad, R. J. (1980). *In sickness and in health: A family physician explores the impact of illness on the family.* Philadelphia: Smith, Kline & French.

McCullogh, D. (March 1983). Mama's boys. *Psychology Today,* 32–38.

McGoldrick, M. (1977). Some data on death and cancer in schizophrenic families. Paper presented at Presymposium Conference of Georgetown Symposium, Washington, D.C.

McGoldrick, M. (1980). The joining of families through marriage: The new couple. In E. A. Carter & M. McGoldrick (Eds.), *The family life cycle: A framework for family therapy.* New York: Gardner Press.

McGoldrick, M. (1982). Ethnicity and family therapy: An overview. In M. McGoldrick, J. K. Pearce, and J. Giordano (Eds.), *Ethnicity and family therapy.* New York: Guilford Press.

McGoldrick Orfanidis, M. (1980). Problems with family genograms. *American Journal of Family Therapy, 7,* 74–76.

McGoldrick, M. & Carter, E. A. (1980). Forming a remarried family. In E. A. Carter & M. McGoldrick (Eds.), *The family life cycle: A framework for family therapy.* New York: Gardner Press.

McGoldrick, M. & Carter, E. A. (1982). The family life cycle. In F. Walsh (Ed.), *Normal family processes.* New York: Guilford Press.

McGoldrick, M., Froom, J., & Snope, F. A standardized genogram: Final report of the NAPCRG committee. Manuscript in preparation.

McGoldrick, M. & Garcia Preto, N. (1984). Ethnic intermarriage: implications for therapy. *Family Process, 23*(3), 347–64.

McGoldrick, M., Pearce, J. K., & Giordano, J. (1982). *Ethnicity and family therapy.* New York: Guilford Press.

McGoldrick, M., Rohrbaugh, M., & Rogers, J. Genograms: Applications in family therapy, family medicine and research. Manuscript in preparation.

McGoldrick, M., Rohrbaugh, M., Weiss, H., Tomm, K., Jolly, W., & Gerson, R. (April 1983). Genograms: Applications in family therapy, family medicine, and research. Panel conducted at the American Orthopsychiatric Association Annual Meeting, Boston.

McGoldrick, M. & Walsh, F. (1983). A systemic view of family history and loss. In L. R. Wolberg & M. L. Aronson (Eds.), *Group and family therapy: 1983.* New York: Brunner/Mazel.

McWhinney, I. R. (1981). *An introduction to family medicine.* New York: Oxford University Press.

Medalie, J. H. (1978). *Family medicine: Principles and applications.* Baltimore: Williams & Wilkins.

Milhorn, H. T. (1981). The genogram: a structured approach to the family history. *Journal of the Mississippi State Medical Association, 22*(10), 250–52.

Minuchin, S. (1974). *Families and family therapy.* Cambridge, MA: Harvard University Press.

Minuchin, S., & Fishman, H. C. (1981). *Family therapy techniques.* Cambridge, MA: Harvard University Press.

Moitoza, E. (1982). Portuguese families. In M. McGoldrick, J. K. Pearce, & J. Giordano (Eds.), *Ethnicity and family therapy.* New York: Guilford Press.

Monte, C. F. (1980). *Beneath the mask: An introduction to theories of personality.* Second Edition. New York: Holt, Rinehart & Winston.

Mueller, P. S., & McGoldrick Orfanidis, M. (1976). A method of cotherapy for schizophrenic families. *Family Process, 15,* 179–92.

Mullins, M. C., & Christie-Seely, J. (1984). Collecting and recording family data – The genogram. In J. Christie-Seely (Ed.), *Working with the family in primary care.* New York: Praeger.

Neugarten, B. (1970). Dynamics of transition of middle age to old age: Adaptation and the life cycle. *Journal of Geriatric Psychiatry, 4,* 71–87.

Papp, P., Silverstein, O., & Carter, E. A. (1973). Family sculpting in preventive work with well families. *Family Process, 12*(2), 197–212.

Patterson, J. M. & McCubbin, H. I. (1983). The impact of family life events and changes on the health of a chronically ill child. *Family Relations,* 255–64.

Paul, N., & Paul, B. (1982). Death and changes in sexual behavior. In F. Walsh (Ed.), *Normal family processes.* New York: Guilford Press.

Paul, N., & Paul, B. (1974). *A marital puzzle.* New York: W. W. Norton.

Pendagast, E. G., & Sherman, C. O. (1977). A guide to the genogram. *The Family, 5,* 3–14.

Rakel, R. E. (1977). *Principles of family medicine.* Philadelphia: W. B. Saunders.

Richardson, H. B. (1945). *Patients have families.* New York: Commonwealth Fund.

Rogers, J. & Durkin, M. (1984). The semi-structured genogram interview: I. Protocol, II. Evaluation. *Family Systems Medicine, 2*(2), 176–187.

Rohrbaugh, M., McGoldrick, M. & Durks, J. (March 1985). Comparison of family patterns following suicide and following another death. Paper presented to the Eastern Psychological Association, Boston.

Rosen, G., Kleinman, A., & Katon, W. (1982). Somatization in family practice: A biopsychosocial approach. *Journal of Family Practice, 14,* 493.

Runck, B. (1977). Families in hard times – a legacy. In E. Corfman (Ed.), *Families today, Vol. 1,* DHHS publication # ADM 79-815. Rockville, MD: National Institute of Mental Health.

Sager, C. J., Brown, H. S., Crohn, H., Engel, T., Rodstein, E., & Walker, L. (1983). *Treating the remarried family.* New York: Brunner/Mazel.

Scheflen, A. (1981). *Levels of schizophrenia.* New York: Brunner/Mazel.

Schmidt, D. D. (1978). The family as the unit of medical care. *Journal of Family Practice, 7,* 303.

Selvini-Palazzoli, M., Boscolo, L., Cecchin, G., & Prata, G. (1980). The problem of the referring person. *Journal of Marital and Family Therapy, 6*(1), 3–9.

Smilkstein, G. (1978). The family APGAR: A proposal for a family function test and its use by physicians. *Journal of Family Practice, 6,* 1231.

Smilkstein, G. (1984). The physician and family function assessment. *Family Systems Medicine, 2*(3), 263–278.

Smoyak, S. (1982). Family systems: Use of genograms as an assessment tool. In I. Clements and D. Buchanan (Eds.) *Family therapy in perspective.* New York: John Wiley & Sons.

Sproul, M. S. & Gallagher, R. M. (1982). The genogram as an aid to crisis intervention. *Journal of Family Practice, 14*(5), 959–60.

Stack, C. B. (1974). *All our kin.* New York: Harper & Row.

Starkey, P. J. (1981). Genograms: a guide to understanding one's own family sytem. *Perspectives in Psychiatric Care, 19,* 164–73.

Steidl, J. H., Finkelstein, O. F., Wexler, J. P., Feigenbaum, H., Kitsen, J., Kliger, A. S., & Quinlan, D. M. (1980). Medical condition, adherence to treatment regimens, and family functioning: Their interactions in patients receiving long-term dialysis treatment. *Archives of General Psychiatry, 37,* 1025.

Stolorow, R. D., & Atwood, G. E. (1979). *Faces in a cloud: Subjectivity in personality theory.* New York: Jason Aronson.

Sutton-Smith, B. & Rosenberg, B. G. (1970). *The sibling.* New York: Holt, Rinehart & Winston.

Toman, W. (1976). *Family constellation* (third edition). New York: Springer.

Wachtel, E. F. (1982). The family psyche over three generations: The genogram revisited. *Journal of Marital and Family Therapy, 8*(3), 335–343.

Walsh, F. (1975). Living for the dead? Schizophrenia and three-generational family relations. Paper presented to the American Psychological Association 38th Annual Meeting.

Walsh, F. (1978). Concurrent grandparent death and birth of schizophrenic offspring: An intriguing finding. *Family Process, 17,* 457–63.

Walsh, F. (1983). The timing of symptoms and critical events in the family life cycle. In H. Liddle (Ed.), *Clinical implications of the family life cycle.* Rockville, Maryland: Aspen Publications.

Widmer, R. B., Cadoret, R S., & North, C. S. (1980). Depression in family practice: Some effects on spouses and children. *Journal of Family Practice, 10,* 45–51.

Woolf, V. V. (1983). Family network systems in transgenerational psychotherapy: The theory, advantages and expanded applications of genograms. *Family Therapy, 10*(3), 119–137.

Wright, L. M., & Leahey, M. (1984). *Nurses and families: A guide to family assessment and intervention.* Philadelphia: F. A. Davis.

BIOGRAPHICAL REFERENCES

Adams Family

Nagel, P. C. (1983). Descent from glory: Four generations of the John Adams family. New York: Oxford University Press.

Adler Family

Adler, A. (1928). Characteristics of 1st, 2nd and 3rd children. *Children, 3*(5).

Adler, A. (1958). *What life should mean to you?* New York: Capricorn Books.

Adler, A. (1964). *Social interest: A challenge to mankind.* New York: Capricorn Books.

Adler, A. (1965). *Understanding human nature,* 6th printing. Greenwich, CT: Fawcett Publications. (Originally published 1927)

Adler, A. (1970). *The education of children.* Chicago: Gateway, Henry Regnery Co. (Originally published 1930)

Adler, A. (1979). *Superiority and social interest: A collection of later writings.* (Eds. H. L. Ansbacher & R. R. Ansbacher). New York: W. W. Norton.

Ansbacher, H. L. (1970). Alfred Adler: A historical perspective. *American Journal of Psychiatry, 127,* 777–782.

Ansbacher, H. L. & Ansbacher, R. R. (1956). *The individual psychology of Alfred Adler.* New York: Harper & Row.

Bottome, P. (1939). *Alfred Adler: A biography.* New York: G. P. Putnam's Sons.

Dreikurs, R. (1967). *Psychodynamics, psychotherapy and counseling.* Chicago: Adler Institute.

Ellenberger, H. F. (1970). *The discovery of the unconscious: The history and evolution of dynamic psychiatry.* New York: Basic Books.

Furtmuller, C. (1979). Alfred Adler: A biographical essay. In H. L. Ansbacher & R. R. Ansbacher (Eds.), *Superiority and social interest: A collection of later writings.* New York: W. W. Norton.

Lieberman, S. (1979). *Transgenerational family therapy.* London: Croom Helm.

Orgler, H. (1963). *Alfred Adler: The man and his work.* New York: New American Library, Mentor.

Rattner, J. (1983). *Alfred Adler.* New York: Frederick Ungar.

Scarf, M. (Feb. 28 1971). Alfred Adler: His ideas are everywhere. *New York Times Magazine.*

Shulman, B. H. (1973). *Contributions to individual psychology.* Chicago: Alfred Adler Institute.

Sperber, M. (1974). *Masks of loneliness: Alfred Adler in perspective.* New York: Macmillan.

Stepansky, P. E. (1983). *In Freud's shadow: Adler in context.* Hillsdale, NJ: The Analytic Press.

Bateson Family

Lipset, D. (1980). *Gregory Bateson: The legacy of a scientist.* Englewood Cliffs, NJ: Prentice Hall.

Bateson, M. C. (1984). *With a daughter's eye: A memoir of Margaret Mead and Gregory Bateson.* New York: William Morrow.

Brockman, J. (Ed.). (1977). *About Bateson.* New York: E. P. Dutton.

Bell Family

Bruce, R. V. (1973). *Bell: Alexander Graham Bell and the conquest of solitude.* Boston: Little, Brown.
Eber, D. H. (1982). *Genius at work: Images of Alexander Graham Bell.* New York: Viking.

Blackwell Family

Horn, M. (1983). "Sisters worthy of respect": Family dynamics and women's roles in the Blackwell family. *Journal of Family History, 8*(4), 367–382.
Horn, M. (1980). Family ties: The Blackwells, a study of the dynamics of family life in nineteenth century America. PhD. Dissertation, Tufts University.

Bronte Family

Gaskell, E. (1975). *The life of Charlotte Bronte.* London: Penguin.
Gerin, W. (1971). *Emily Bronte: A biography.* London: Oxford University Press.
Hanson, L. & Hanson, E. (1967). *The four Brontes.* New York: Archon Press.
Hopkins, A. B. (1958). *The father of the Brontes.* Baltimore: Johns Hopkins Press.
Lane, M. (1969). *The Bronte story.* London: Fontana.
Lock, J. & Dixon, W. T. (1965). *A man of sorrow: The life, letters, and times of Reverend Patrick Bronte.* Westport, CT: Meckler Books.
Mackay, A. M. (1897). *The Brontes: Fact and fiction.* New York: Dodd, Mead.
Moglen, H. (1984). *Charlotte Bronte: The self conceived.* Madison: University of Wisconsin Press.
Peters, M. (1974). *An enigma of Brontes.* New York: St. Martin's Press.
Winnifith, T. Z. (1977). *The Brontes and their background: Romance and reality.* New York: Collier.

Callas Family

Stassinopoulos, A. (1981). *Maria Callas: The woman behind the legend.* New York: Simon & Schuster.

Chaplin Family

Chaplin, C. (1964). *My autobiography.* New York: Simon and Schuster.
Chaplin, C., Jr. (1960). *My father, Charlie Chaplin.* New York: Random House.
McCabe, J. (1978). *Charlie Chaplin.* New York: Doubleday.

Churchill Family

Brendon, P. (1984). *Winston Churchill.* New York: Harper & Row.
Churchill, R. S. (1966). *Winston S. Churchill: Youth 1874-1900.* Boston: Houghton Mifflin.
Gilbert, M. (1980). *Churchill.* Garden City, New York: Doubleday.
Manchester, W. (1983). *The last lion: Winston Spencer Churchill* (Vol. 1). Boston: Little, Brown.
Martin, R. G. (1972). *Jennie: The life of Lady Randolph Churchill* (Vols. 1-2). New York: Signet.
Payne, R. (1974). *The great man: A portrait of Winston Churchill.* New York: Coward, McCann & Goeghegan, Inc.

Einstein Family

Clark, R. W. (1971). *Einstein: The life and times.* New York: Avon.
French, A. P. (Ed.). (1979). *Einstein: A centenary volume.* Cambridge, MA: Harvard University Press.
Pais, A. (1982). *The science and the life of Albert Einstein.* New York: Oxford University Press.
Sayen, J. (1985). *Einstein in America.* New York: Crown Publishers Inc.

Fitzgerald Family

Milford, N. (1970). *Zelda, A biography.* New York: Harper & Row.
Stavola, T. J. (1979). *Scott Fitzgerald: Crisis in American identity.* Totowa, NJ: Barnes & Noble.
Turnbull, A. (1962). *Scott Fitzgerald.* New York: Charles Scribner's Sons.

Fonda Family

Guiles, F. L. (1981). *Jane Fonda: The actress in her time.* New York: Pinnacle.
Hayward, B. (1977). *Haywire.* New York: Alfred Knopf.
Kiernan, T. (1973). *Jane: An intimate biography of Jane Fonda.* New York: Putnam.
Sheed, W. (1982). *Clare Booth Luce.* New York: E. P. Dutton.
Springer, J. (1970). *The Fondas.* Seacaucus: Citadel.
Teichman, H. (1981). *Fonda: My life.* New York: New American Library.

Freud Family

Interviews with Hella Bernays and Edward Bernays, niece and nephew of Freud.
Bank, S. & Kahn, M. D. (1980). Freudian siblings. *Psychoanalytic Review, 67,* 493–504.
Bernays, Anna Freud. (Nov. 1940) My brother Sigmund Freud. *The American Mercury,* 336–340.
Bernays, E. L. (1965). *Biography of an idea.* New York: Simon & Schuster.
Clark, C. W. (1980). *Freud: The man and the cause.* London: Jonathan Cape and Weidenfeld & Nicolson.
Eissler, K. R. (1978). *Sigmund Freud: His life in pictures and words.* New York: Helen and Kurt Wolff Books, Harcourt Brace Jovanovich.
Engelman, Edmund. (1976). *Berggasse 19.* New York: Basic Books.
Freeman, L. & Strean, H. S. (1981). *Freud and women.* New York: Frederick Ungar.
Freud, M. (1958). *Sigmund Freud: Man and father.* New York: Vanguard.
Freud Lowenstein, S. (1980). Book review: *Freud und sein Vater. Family Process, 19*(2), 307–13.
Fromm, E. (1959). *Sigmund Freud's mission.* New York: Grove.
Glicklhorn, R. (1969). The Freiberg period of the Freud family. *Journal of the History of Medicine, 24,* 37–43.
Jones, E. (1953–57). *The life and work of Sigmund Freud* (3 Volumes). New York: Basic Books.
Krüll, M. (1979). *Freud und sein Vater.* Munich: Verlag C. H. Beck.
Natenberg, M. (1955). *The case history of Sigmund Freud: A psycho-biography.* Chicago: Regent House.
Roazen, P. (1975). *Freud and his followers.* New York: Alfred A. Knopf.
Wallechinsky, D. & Wallace, I. (1975). *The people's almanac.* New York: Harper & Row.

Hepburn Family

Carey, G. (1983). *Katherine Hepburn: A Hollywood yankee.* New York: Dell.
Higham, C. (1975). *Kate: The life of Katherine Hepburn.* New York: New American Library.

Jefferson Family

Binger, C. (1970). *Thomas Jefferson: A well-tempered mind.* New York: W. W. Norton.
Brodie, F. M. (1974). *Thomas Jefferson: An intimate history.* New York: W. W. Norton.
Fleming, T. J. (1969). *The man from Monticello.* New York: William Morrow & Co.

Jung Family

Brome, V. (1981). *Jung: Man and myth.* New York: Atheneum.
Hannah, B. (1981). *Jung: His life and work; A biographical memoir.* New York: Perigee, Putnam Books.

Jung, C. G. (1961). *Memories, dreams, reflections* (Recorded and edited by Aniela Jaffe, translated by R. Winston & C. Winston). New York: Vintage Books.
Stern, P. J. (1976). *C. G. Jung: The haunted prophet*. New York: Delta, Dell Publishers.

Kennedy Family

Collier, P., & Horowitz, D. (1984). *The Kennedys: An American drama*. New York: Summit Books.
Davis, J. (1984). *The Kennedys: Dynasty and disaster 1848–1983*. New York: McGraw-Hill.
Kennedy, R. (1974). *Times to remember*. New York: Bantam.
Wills, G. (1981). *The Kennedy imprisonment*. New York: Pocket Books.

King Family

King, M. L., Sr., with C. Riely (1980). *Daddy King, an autobiography*. New York: William Morrow.
Oates, S. B. (1982). *Let the trumpet sound, the life of Martin Luther King, Jr.* New York: Harper & Row.

Mead Family

Bateson, M. C. (1984). *With a daughter's eye: A memoir of Margaret Mead and Gregory Bateson*. New York: William Morrow.
Cassidy, R. (1981). *Margaret Mead: A voice for the century*. New York: Universe Books.
Howard, J. (1984). *Margaret Mead: A life*. New York: Simon & Schuster.
Mead, M. (1972). *Blackberry winter*. New York: Washington Square Press.
Rice, E. (1979). *Margaret Mead*. New York: Harper & Row.

Nehru-Ghandi Family

Ali, T. (1985). *An indian dynasty*. New York: G. P. Putnam's Sons.
Nehru, J. (1941). *Toward freedom: The autobiography of Jawaharlal Nehru*. New York: John Day Co.
Nehru Huthessing, K., with Hatch, A. (1967). *We Nehrus*. New York: Holt, Rinehart & Winston.
Morses, F. (1956). *Jawaharlal Nehru: A biography*. New York: Macmillan.

O'Neill Family

Gelb, A. & Gelb, B. (1970). *O'Neill*. New York: Harper & Row.
O'Neill, E. (1955). *Long day's journey into night*. New Haven: Yale University Press.
Sheafer, L. (1968). *Son and playwright*. Boston: Little, Brown, & Co.
Sheafer, L. (1973). *Son and artist*. Boston: Little, Brown, & Co.

Reich Family

Mann, W. E., & Hoffman, E. (1980). *The man who dreamed of tomorrow: The life and thought of Wilhelm Reich*. Los Angeles: J. P. Tarcher, Inc.
Reich, I. O. (1969). *Wilhelm Reich: A personal biography*. New York: Avon.
Sharaf, M. (1983). *Fury on earth: A biography of Wilhelm Reich*. New York: St. Martins.
Wilson, C. (1981). *The quest for Wilhelm Reich: A critical biography*. Garden City, New York: Anchor Press/Doubleday.

Roosevelt Family

Lash, J. P. (1971). *Eleanor and Franklin*. New York: W. W. Norton.
Miller, N. (1979). *The Roosevelt chronicles*. Garden City, NY: Doubleday.

Miller, N. (1983). *FDR: An intimate biography*. Garden City, NY: Doubleday.

Youngs, W. T. (1985). *Eleanor Roosevelt: A personal and public life*. Boston: Little, Brown, & Co.

Shaw/Payne-Townshend Families

Colbourne, M. (1949). *The real Bernard Shaw*. New York: Philosophical Library.

Dervin, D. (1975). *Bernard Shaw: A psychological study*. Lewisberg, PA: Bucknell University Press.

Dunbar, J. (1963). *Mrs. G. B. S.: A portrait*. New York: Harper & Row.

Smith, J. P. (1965). *The unrepentant pilgrim: A study of the development of Bernard Shaw*. Boston: Houghton Mifflin.

Sullivan Family

Chapman, A. H. (1976). *Harry Stack Sullivan: The man and his work, his psychiatry and its relevance to current American dilemmas*. New York: Putnam.

Perry, H. S. (1982). *Psychiatrist of America: The life of Harry Stack Sullivan*. Cambridge, MA: The Belknap Press of Harvard University Press.

Taylor/Burton

Ferris, P. (1981). *Richard Burton*. New York: Coward, McCann & Geoghegan.

Kelley, K. (1981). *Elizabeth Taylor: The last star*. New York: Simon & Schuster.

Woolf Family

Bell, Q. (1972). *Virginia Woolf: A biography*. New York: Harcourt & Brace.

INDEX